PRACTICING FAITH

Also by Berry Simpson

Running With God
Retreating With God
Remodeled
Trail Markers

PRACTICING FAITH
Seeking God Through this Season of Life

Berry Simpson

stonefoot media
Midland, Texas

Practicing Faith
Copyright © 2020 by Berry Simpson
All rights reserved. No part of this publication may be reproduced, stored in a retrieval system, or transmitted in any form or by any means—electronic, mechanical, photocopy, recording, or any other—except for brief quotations in printed reviews, without the prior permission of the authors.

All Scripture quotations, unless otherwise indicated, are taken from the Holy Bible, New International Version®, NIV®. Copyright ©1973, 1978, 1984, 2011 by Biblica, Inc.™ Used by permission of Zondervan. All rights reserved worldwide. www.zondervan.com The "NIV" and "New International Version" are trademarks registered in the United States Patent and Trademark Office by Biblica, Inc.™

Scripture quotations marked MSG are taken from THE MESSAGE, copyright © 1993, 2002, 2018 by Eugene H. Peterson. Used by permission of NavPress. All rights reserved. Represented by Tyndale House Publishers, a Division of Tyndale House Ministries.

Scripture quotations designated NASB are taken from the New American Standard Bible® (NASB). Copyright © 1960, 1962, 1963, 1968, 1971, 1972, 1973,1975, 1977, 1995 by The Lockman Foundation. Used by permission. www.Lockman.org.

Scripture quotations designated NLT are taken from the Holy Bible, New Living Translation. Copyright ©1996, 2004, 2007, 2013, 2015 by Tyndale House Foundation. Used by permission of Tyndale House Publishers, Inc., Carol Stream, Illinois 60188. All rights reserved.

Scripture quotations designated "Phillips" are taken from The New Testament in Modern English by J. B Phillips. Copyright © 1958, 1960, 1972 by J. B. Phillips. Copyright renewed © 1986, 1988 by Vera M. Phillips.

Web addresses shown were accurate and functioning at the time this book went to print. The author does not vouch for their continued viability.

Editor: Bob Hartig
Cover design: Darrell Dunton

Book Layout © 2017 BookDesignTemplates.com

Practicing Faith / Berry Simpson. -- 1st ed.
ISBN 978-0-9831400-8-5

This book is dedicated to
Cyndi Simpson – without you I would have little interest in writing, or cycling, or hiking, or even life itself.
and
Rabon Bewley - you inspired this book with your talk during our Iron Men's retreat in 2018, titled "Practicing Faith and How You Swing It." It was a direct hit to two of my most sensitive spots: daily practice and music. It was the majority of what I thought about, wrote about, and talked about, for the next two years.

Contents

Preface ix
Acknowledgments xi
Introduction 1
Family: Roots of Hope 11
Eulogy and Legacy 23
Ongoing Hope 33
Love for a Lifetime 43
Growing through Failure 59
Living with New Knees 67
Moving My Feet 73
Connecting on the Trail 79
What I Learn from Cycling 91
Telling Stories of Life 101
Experiencing the Sacred 111
Grace Abounds 117
Not On My Own 131
A Less Busy Heart 139
Keep Exploring 149
Practicing Faith 163
Still Learning New Tricks 173
What We Learned from a Good Dog 189
Leaning Forward 199
About the Author 205
Notes 207

Preface

Perhaps the greatest legacy we can leave from our work is . . . the passing on of a sense of sheer privilege, of having found a road, a way to follow, and then having been allowed to walk it, often with others, with all its difficulties and minor triumphs; the underlying primary gift, of having been a full participant in the conversation.
—David Whyte

When I first started writing *Practicing Faith*, I thought I would end up with a how-to book full of historical perspectives, advice from my sixty-four years, and practical suggestions for adding spiritual practices to your life. But as I did my research, I realized how many quality books along those lines are already available, many of them on my own library shelf and all of them better than I could write.

Since all my writing begins from personal stories, I decided that, instead of teaching techniques, I would dive deep into how practicing faith has made my life, and how doing so looks and feels to me. This is a book of stories, and while they are recorded chronologically in my journals, I seldom remember them that way. Recall can be chaotic and messy, so expect the timeline to leap forward and backward.

I am writing to describe what has been happening and what I've been learning and experiencing, but really what comes out is what I want to be, how I want to live, what I want to learn and experience next.

Acknowledgments

I want to say thanks to some of the people who made this book possible:

Bob Hartig from Hastings, Michigan, who edited my text and made it readable. Book after book, I've been amazed how well he knows what I meant to say better than I said it. You can find him at *thecopyfox.com*.

Darrell Dunton with Admarc in Midland, Texas, designed the cover. My friend and loyal reader for many years, he once encouraged me to turn my essays into books and kept pushing me to make sure it really happened. We all need friends who push us into doing what we know we should do.

Alexie Patane, Ravenlily Photography, Denver, CO, took the back-cover photo, at Bear Trap Ranch, CO.

Eszter Lesták took the *About the Author* photo, at a Metro Big Band concert in Budapest, Hungary

Clark Moreland and Jeff Kuhnhenn, founding members of our writer's group, the MidInklings.

Introduction

A few of us were sitting around a restaurant table discussing how we could become better teachers when John gave us a challenge: "Find five words that describe who you are, who you want to be, and the mission and impact you want for your life."

I found a long list of words left over from a previous retreat, and I used it to select my five words: relevant, hope, authentic, sharing, and student. I wrote each of them on a small scrap of paper, shuffled the stack, wrote them down in order, and tried to build a sentence with them.

I did this over and over, reshuffling and rewriting, until I had a sentence that felt correct and authentic. My five words, in sentence form, were: Be a man of hope, living an authentic life, sharing what I learn, and staying culturally relevant as a lifelong student of significant things.

Since doing the exercise and thinking more about this sentence and my five words, I've realized the single most important word for me is sharing. Sharing what I've learned is the prime motivator of my life.

Psalm 66:16 says, "Come and hear, all you who fear God; let me tell what he has done for me." That's what I want to do, tell stories of what God has done for me.

This urge to tell stories is why I write, defines my teaching style, and describes the best of my projects while I was in city government. It is my favorite part of being a church deacon and in church leadership. It is the reason I want to publish. It is who I am, a storyteller.

I want my stories to be your invitation to join, to go deeper with God. I hope they help you notice and embrace the moments of daily life when God pulls you in closer. My challenge to you is this: to see God's hand in everything.

♦ ♦ ♦ ♦ ♦

One December evening, just last winter, I was about two miles into my three-mile run when I heard the voice in my head say, "It wasn't for you."

I had been listening to a podcast about trail running, and the speaker was discussing how our fear of failure controls so many of our thoughts and actions. As so often happens, the story I was hearing wasn't the same story my brain landed on. Suddenly I was back in the 1980s and a story I'd been telling myself for thirty years: "You weren't good enough."

I was working in Midland, Texas, for a major oil company as district engineer, a job I was proud of and a job I loved. Business had been booming, still riding the wave of the 1970s when oil reached a peak price of $35 a barrel, the equivalent of $102 in today's dollars. It was a great time to be in oil and gas. Until suddenly it wasn't.

In a moment, oil prices went into worldwide freefall, eventually dropping to $8 per barrel and wreaking havoc on all of us. In Midland, companies were going bankrupt sequentially, which in turn caused six banks to fail.

And then the unthinkable happened: First National Bank, the flagship bank and pride of Midland, failed in spite of holding $1.3 billion in assets.

The FDIC was so busy in Midland liquidating banks and businesses that they set up shop in a building near Clay Desta, now known as the Apache Building but which people like me who survived that era still refer to as the FDIC Building. The FDIC eventually became Midland County's third-largest employer.

I had friends all over town who were laid off or lost their businesses. Every Sunday at church we heard the update: who was looking for work, who was in trouble, who was moving away. One of my best friends, a geologist, got a job slicing meat at a grocery store, so he got to keep his house.

In the middle of all this terrible news, I got a phone call from the vice-president of production in Tulsa, asking me to consider taking a transfer to our office in Rio Vista, California. While friends were losing their jobs, I was being offered a promotion.

On paper it was a parallel transfer, equivalent to the job I already had, but with respect to budget and activity and company visibility, it was a big opportunity to step up the corporate ladder. It would be a high-profile position with unlimited opportunity to keep moving up, and I was honored to be offered the chance.

Cyndi and I traveled to Lodi, California, (made famous by John Fogerty and Credence Clearwater Revival) to look around the town and meet my future coworkers. The main two things we noticed were the nonexistence of edible Mexican food and the shockingly high real estate prices. It was frightening. While the housing market in Midland had collapsed, the market in central California was booming.

We couldn't afford anything in Lodi that was a place we'd want to live in and raise our six-year-old son and three-year-old daughter. In addition, we couldn't sell our house in Midland for enough to pay off the mortgage. Real estate prices had fallen so quickly that we were $30,000 upside down in our mortgage. It would've taken us a lifetime to recover from a financial hit like that.

However, despite all that, we were looking forward to the change and doing whatever we could to make the details work out. I was so excited about the opportunity in California that I didn't understand the long-lasting economic price we'd have to pay.

To prepare for the move, we'd sold our extra car, which wouldn't have passed California emission standards, and Cyndi quit her job. We'd attended several going-away parties and even accepted gifts. We were ready to go.

Until the end of May.

I was in a quarterly production meeting in Seminole, Texas, when the regional manager pulled me aside and told me my transfer was going to be delayed for a while. He said the VPs in the meeting didn't really know who I was, and it would be a good idea for me to hang out with them and try to make a good impression. I was stunned. I'd planned to leave for California the next day. Only now I was supposed to enter some corporate fraternity rush to make a good impression to earn the position I'd already been offered and that I was clearly qualified for. It was humiliating.

The delay stretched across the summer, leaving us feeling homeless and unneeded. I had little to work on since I'd passed my projects on to the other engineers in the office. Every week I'd hear the same thing from the regional manager: "Not yet, we'll let you know."

Finally, four months later in September, the regional manager told me the entire transfer had been canceled. The future was over. When I asked him why, and did I do something wrong, he just looked away and wouldn't answer. All I could get from him was a mumble about eight-dollar oil. I knew that was part of it but not the entire story. No matter how bad the oil prices, the company would move someone to California, just not us.

Months later I understood that my transfer was caught up in a battle between two vice presidents, and my guy lost, He retired a few months later. But I was left to assume it was all my fault. I didn't measure up in the eyes of senior management. I wasn't good enough as an engineer. I would never be one of the big boys, one of the cool kids.

Cyndi and I had said goodbye to so many close friends, it was embarrassing to still be in town. People saw us at church and asked, "Are you still here? We thought you'd moved."

Today, when we look back on those years, we see that our closest friends after "the move" were different people than before. It was too awkward to reconnect and start over.

I never really recovered. After that day, I didn't work as late or work as hard as before. My imagination and creativity—my best assets—went to other ventures outside my job. I still did good engineering work, but it was at 75 percent instead of 120 percent.

Why did I give up? Because the way I saw it, I got my turn and did my best, and I was smart and clever, but I got slammed by the company. They took away the offer and gave it to someone else. When I realized my best stuff didn't have a chance to succeed, I relaxed and quit playing along. In that moment, I lost interest in the corporate game.

And here's another thing. My friends were losing their jobs, but I was still working and well-paid. I had a bit of survivor's guilt, so I kept all my pain and disappointment inside. It didn't seem manly to complain about a missed promotion when my friends were losing their homes.

I continued working for the same company until they sold all their Midland assets during the 1994 oil price downturn and I was laid off. I was unemployed for the next two years.

Since then I've continued to work in the oil and gas industry in Midland as a contract engineer or engineering consultant for a dozen different companies. I love living in Midland and working in Midland, but I have no desire to move up anybody's corporate ladder.

If you'd asked, I would have told you I had outgrown the resentment that came from that career-changing incident. That my worst day was long behind me.

That is, until one dark December night when I understood this thirty-year-old story was still haunting me.

When I heard those words in my head, "It wasn't for you," it did more than take me back to 1986. It also opened up my eyes to the different life I now live.

In that moment, in that instance, as I was running west alongside Mike Black's long fence on Mockingbird between Alysheba Lane and A Street, I finally realized the answer to my story was not the one I'd been telling myself for thirty years. I had been wrong. I was not held back by a short-sighted employer, as I'd thought. Instead, I'd been set free. The promotion I wanted, the opportunity I craved, might've been a good career move, but it wasn't right for me. It wasn't the best future for our family.

Here's the thing: if the job had worked out and we'd made the move, odds are I would be an upper-level manager today in that same major oil company, pulling down big dollars, living in a giant house, and spending lavishly on my lovely wife.

But what would be the effect of our lives besides oil and gas? Where would our lasting impact be? Where would our significance be?

That December night, during my last mile running home, I looked back at the important things in our lives that we would have missed had we made the move to California in 1986.

The ministries we are involved in today would never have happened, and neither would their life-changing effect on people around us.

The twelve years I spent in city government, and all the amazing projects I helped work on, would not have been possible had we moved.

The true story was this: I hadn't been jilted by my company. I had been saved by God. The corporate climb wasn't for me. My place was to stay in Midland and invest in the people entrusted to us. I could never have made that decision on my own. I needed God's intervention. I needed to be set free.

In his book The Second Mountain, David Brooks described the two mountains of life. The first mountain is mostly about success and the second about significance. Brooks describes how people make the transition from the one to the other: "People get knocked off that [first] mountain by some failure. Something happens to their career, their family, or their reputation."[1]

I didn't understand it at the time, but the offer of a new job, and then the subsequent quick loss of that gift, began my transition from the first mountain to the second. That second mountain is my life's mission for the years God yet grants me:

> *Be a man of hope,*
> *living an authentic life, sharing what I learn,*
> *and staying culturally relevant*
> *as a lifelong student of significant things.*

Part One

Be a Man of HOPE

Chapter 1

Family: Roots of Hope

I learned to live in hope from my family—from my mom and dad, grandparents, aunts and uncles, and cousins. My courage to live a life of hope came from Cyndi, my wife, and Byron and Katie, my son and daughter. And my granddaughters. For me, family gave me hope.

♦ ♦ ♦ ♦ ♦

Our family didn't come from Baptist royalty, and none of us will ever make the Baptist hall of fame. But we were observant. We went to church a minimum of three times a week, twice on Sunday and once on Wednesday. We went to a variety of regional monthly meetings. We went to summer camps—both my mom and my dad ran camps for years and years, girls' camps and boys' camps—at Paisano Baptist Encampment[2] near Alpine, Texas. And we spent vacations at Glorieta Baptist Assembly[3] near Santa Fe, New Mexico. I grew up going to Sunday school, Vacation Bible School, Sunbeams, Royal Ambassadors, youth choir, all of them all the time.

My family have been members of one Baptist church after another my entire life. And during my college years, when many young adults rebel against the practices of their parents, my life and faith were transformed by the ministry of the Baptist Student Union (now Baptist Collegiate Ministry)[4] in Norman.

♦ ♦ ♦ ♦ ♦

There was a long lineage of preachers in my mom's family. My grandfather Roy Haynes pastored small rural churches in West Texas and New Mexico—places like Ira, Gail, Ackerly, and Loco Hills. I spent several weeks every summer with them, meaning I attended countless weddings and funerals of people and families I didn't know. (Later, when I was in high school, a classmate died in an auto accident, and I was surprised to learn how many of my friends had never been to a funeral.)

Music and church are the deepest roots of my life. When my mom was a senior in high school in Ackerly, she was the church pianist. During a week-long revival meeting, two young students, boys from Howard Payne College, came to Ackerly, one to do the preaching and the other, my dad, to lead the music. My mom and dad found each other playing and singing church music and fell in love.

Unlike many who write about their life in church, I had a grand and formative experience. I don't remember it ever feeling burdensome or oppressive. I never felt a judgmental spirit or atmosphere as described by so many others who grew up in church. I took from my observant upbringing an appreciation of love and grace and permanent love of Jesus.

♦ ♦ ♦ ♦ ♦

These were my comments on Monday, August 4, 2014, at the memorial service for my mother, Wanda Lenelle Simpson, after she died from complications brought on by Alzheimer's Disease.

Psalm 66:16 says, "Come and hear, all you who fear God; let me tell you what he has done for me."

I remember—growing up—there was always music in the house. Mom played piano and we always had a piano in our house. We listened to a lot of music, in those days mostly gospel quartets and choir music.

Since we attended small churches, Mom and Dad were the entire worship team. My dad led the music, and my mom played the piano or organ.

Back in those days we had special music (a solo) every Sunday. Only in those small churches there weren't many good soloists available, so I was often encouraged (instructed) to play trombone specials. I stayed in the regular rotation.

I don't know if my brother Carroll played any drum solos—that would've been very cool—but he was twelve years younger than me, so I was already away from home by then.

Mom paid the price for raising two musicians. Not only the cash price for buying trombones and drums and lessons, but the price of having both Carroll and me practicing at all hours of the day and night. She even put up with rock band rehearsals in the living room that vibrated pictures off the shelves.

I remember in 1974, just after I graduated from high school, how she heard of an opening for a bass trombone player in the Continental Singers, and she would not leave me alone until I applied and was accepted. I went on to play with that same group for three summers.

And later, she always bragged about Carroll playing drums for money with grown-up musicians when he was only in high school. And she was so proud of him even though he was playing in bars. This was not a small concession for her.

Music was one of Mom's last visible connections with the outside world. The nursing attendants in the Alzheimer's Unit where she lived said she would mouth the words of hymns during music time, long after she was capable of having a regular conversation.

In December 2011, Mom and Dad moved from Hobbs, New Mexico, to Midland, Texas. They'd lived in Hobbs for forty-two years, which means they'd accumulated a lot of stuff. There were a lot of boxes to fill and move, and all of those boxes ended up in my garage. Along with furniture and clothes and file cabinets.

In the file cabinets I found drawer after drawer of files labeled: Fashion Show, GA Presentation, WMU business local, WMU business regional, WMU business state-wide. And each category had multiple files, one for each year.

They were all meticulously organized and documented, including photos and samples of programs and handouts. They were more than structural business files; they represented a life devoted to service to church and women's ministries. They were investments into people and the work of God.

Any time you go to a worship service that opens your heart to God, or go to a workshop where you learn significant truths, or attend an event where you meet real live missionaries, or go to a fashion show that raises money and awareness for God's work, or go to a GA [Girls in Action] coronation and see God's working in the hearts of young girls . . . behind every event like that, there is a file cabinet full of ideas.

That was my mom for over sixty years.

Something else I discovered while packing and unpacking boxes were stacks of prayer journals. Inside those journals I found all our names, handwritten, over and over. Mom wasn't the type to talk out loud about her spirituality, but those journals showed how she worked it out, day after day.

One of my favorite Bible passages about family, is Isaiah 51:1[5] . . . "Listen to me, all you who are serious about right living and committed to seeking God. Ponder the rock from which you were cut, the quarry from which you were dug."

I come from quality rock. I was cut from a deep rich quarry of musicians and preachers and deacons and WMU [Woman's Missionary Union] leaders and camp directors. And every year I'm more and more aware of the strength that comes from that quarry.

If there is anything in my life that is true, noble, right, pure, lovely, admirable, excellent, or praiseworthy, it is because I was raised by godly parents who poured their life into me.

Because of my mom and dad, there has never been a time in my life when I didn't hear the words of Jesus, when I wasn't surrounded by faithful church people, or when I didn't witness my parents actively engaged in the work of the church.

But it isn't enough to brag about a strong family background. We cannot live our lives only for ourselves. We are the quarry from which our children and grandchildren are cut, and we have the obligation to pass on the same strength we received.

So my challenge to you is this: Take a look at your life and the legacy you are building. What's in your file cabinet?

Because, just like my mom, how you live ... matters for a long time.

♦ ♦ ♦ ♦ ♦

Late that Monday evening after my mom's memorial service, I received this email from my Dad: "If ever I made a suggestion for a journal, this would be the time—'It's been a good day.' I have been asleep for an hour and woke up with that on my mind. It's the last thing you said to me after we delivered the flowers and you dropped me off."

He sent that message only hours after attending the memorial honoring my mom, his wife of fifty-nine years, who died five days earlier.

He considered it a good day.

Before I drove Dad home that evening, we spent several hours with friends who came to our house to share comfort. We ate lots of food furnished by Dad's Sunday school class. They took excellent care of us—a network of support that instantly jumped into action to minister to our family.

Some of the friends who joined us were new friends, many were family, and some friends went back more than sixty years. They filled the entire weekend with hope and faith and love.

We often take the support we get from other Christians for granted because we see it in action so often. We know that if a disaster strikes our family, we can make one or two phone calls and a hundred people will be holding us and praying for us and serving us. Most Christians have the same confidence in that safety net—but what about the rest of the world? I'm sure there are groups besides churches who do this sort of thing for each other, but I don't see them in action the way I've seen Sunday school classes minister to one another.

During those days before Mom's memorial service, I was reminded by several people that "your mother is in a better place." And it's a true statement, one my family believes so deeply that we never actually discussed it. It was too obvious, as in "Everybody knows that."

Instead, our talk centered on how my mom lived during the seventy-two years before Alzheimer's took over. Everybody knew without a doubt she was with God in heaven. So we told stories about her life and looked at photos and laughed together.

I'll be honest. I didn't intend to write about this again. I prefer to move ahead in joy and discover what adventure comes next. But I couldn't resist my dad's suggestion. Like he said, "It was a good day."

♦ ♦ ♦ ♦ ♦

"What are you doing early Thursday morning?" asked my dad. "Are you busy?"

"I'm teaching my Iron Men class at church. It's our first session of 2016, and we meet at 6:30 a.m."

"OK. I guess you're busy."

"Why are you asking?"

"I need a ride to the hospital at 6:00 a.m."

"Can you be more specific?"

"I'm having surgery on my carotid artery. You know—the one they've all been worrying about because of my high blood pressure. They're going to do a Roto-Rooter on it."

"You asked if I was busy before telling me you're having surgery? Don't you have that backwards?"

"Well, maybe."

We had this conversation on our way to Saturday lunch at Rosa's with Cyndi. Over our enchiladas we worked out a satisfactory plan where Cyndi would drive Dad to the hospital at 6:00, and I would come as soon as I was finished with my class.

I asked, "Have you told your Sunday school class you are having surgery next week?"

"No, I don't want to be one of those people who have something wrong with them every week."

"Have you mentioned anything before now?"

"Well, no."

"I think you're safe. But you're going to get into trouble if you don't mention it. They want to take care of you because they love you. That's the job of Sunday school classes, to take care of each other."

"OK."

It's our family's way to fly low under the radar, to not complain, to keep our problems to ourselves. Not because we are especially tough or because we are martyrs—we just don't want to be a lot of trouble. And we don't need much attention to feel accepted and loved.

I had to learn how to let other people take care of me. It took a deliberate change in my thinking to allow people to serve me. It didn't come naturally. I thought, as a leader and a teacher, that serving was my job. I was uncomfortable on the other side of service.

Even last summer after knee replacement surgeries, I tried doing everything myself before asking Cyndi for help. I don't think it was because I was so stubborn; it simply didn't occur to me that I shouldn't try it myself first. After all, how else would I learn my own limits?

Cyndi and I both have had to learn to let other people help us. Allowing other people to serve us is a significant part of leadership, a step forward in spiritual maturity. We've had to stand down and relax, and it hasn't been easy.

A few years back, I was on a Guadalupe Mountains backpacking trip with my friend David Nobles. It was the first day of the trip, and we were carrying our heavy packs up Tejas Trail, which is four miles long and climbs 3,000 feet in elevation. For some reason, I started falling apart about halfway up, getting short-winded, faint, and sick to my stomach. I was taking way too many long rest breaks. So, David hustled up to the top of the ridge, dropped his pack on the ground, then came back to help me carry mine. I had done the same for other men on several occasions, but I'd never needed that sort of help myself. It would have been embarrassing if I hadn't been so grateful.

Here's the thing: If all we do in life is carry for others and never allow them to carry for us, that really isn't relationship. If all we do is give and never receive, we must wonder about our motives. Are we truly serving the needs of others or feeding the needs of our own ego? We must be willing to receive if we expect to know the grace of God. Only empty-handed people can understand grace. Only vulnerable leaders can understand grace.

So, Thursday morning I visited my dad about an hour after his surgery, when he was just coming around from the anesthesia. A nurse followed me into the room and said, "Mr. Simpson, I need to take a blood sample."

"You'll have to ask the last nurse who was in here. She got the last of my blood."

That's another family trait I learned from my dad—there is always a joke.

♦ ♦ ♦ ♦ ♦

This was my last exchange with Dad when I could be certain I understood what he was trying to say:

"How do you feel this morning?"

"I feel great!"

He was propped up in a hospital chair, couldn't open his eyes, couldn't swallow. Yet he wasn't complaining.

"What have you been doing all morning?"

"We had a volleyball tournament. Our team won."

After his funeral, a lot of people asked, "What were your father's last words?"

"Well, dad was cracking jokes, making people smile, not complaining, and enjoying what he could of the life he had left."

That's how I want to go. It seems profound to me.

I had lunch with my dad at least once a week for the past five years, and while we often said nothing to each other, like men tend to do, we never ran out of things to talk about. I am content that he and I said everything that needed to be said between us. There was nothing left to settle, explain, justify, defend, or forgive. We just had fun together.

For most of my life, I thought of Mom as my biggest influence. I followed her structured life, her love for reading, her search for quiet and solitude, her temperament, and her personality.

Music and humor came from my dad, but little else. However, the more I've listened to stories and comments from friends over the past weeks, I've realized Dad's significant imprint on my life. Even though we were quite different men, I am grateful for what I have of my father in me.

I have been blessed in the best way possible: both my parents loved me, were proud of me, and believed in me, every day of my life. My mom bragged about me even when she was living in the Alzheimer's Unit. Even when I wasn't sure she remembered my name, her eyes would light up every time I came close to her. And my dad continued to tell stories about me to his friends all the way to the end. I know this because those stories have been coming back to me lately from those very same people.

I realize maybe that wasn't your life. Maybe you never had that sort of relationship with your parents or with any of your family.

If that's your story, I'm truly sorry. You cannot change the past, but you can change the future. You can give your children, grandchildren, great-grandchildren, and generations you will never meet a new story to tell. You can change your family's future by deciding to love unconditionally, respect unconditionally, and believe unconditionally.

Chapter 2

Eulogy and Legacy

Written Thursday, March 30, 2017.

We're planning to move my dad into hospice care tonight. I don't expect him to last much longer. He hasn't been able to swallow food or liquids in a week, can't open his eyes, can barely communicate, and wrestles with breathing. He is eighty-eight years old. It's time to let him go home.

Six days ago, he fell in his apartment. I dropped by to take him to lunch and found him flat on his back on the kitchen floor.

"Are you OK, Dad?"

"Sure. I just decided to take a nap."

He couldn't tell me how long he'd been down on the floor.

We didn't know until later, but three weeks before he apparently had a series of small strokes that slowed his gait even more than it was, affected his ability to balance on his bicycle, and rendered his once-dependable legs weak and unstable. He asked me to get him a walker, one with wheels and a bench, which I initially resisted because I wasn't ready to see him with one. For some reason I can't defend or explain, I was more concerned with my own feelings of physical vulnerability than his personal safety.

Three months ago, I signed both of us up for a men's ski trip sponsored by our church. It was his idea. I wondered about the wisdom of turning an eighty-eight-year-old man loose on the slopes. "Are you sure you can do this?" I asked.

"We'll find out."

Seven months ago, Dad and I rode our bikes for eight laps around Manor Park, the gated retirement village where he's lived since 2011, in honor of his eighty-eighth birthday. I tried to talk him into riding eight-eight laps. "No way."

Three years ago, my Mom died after a long slide into Alzheimer's. I drove Dad home after the funeral with a car full of flowers he wanted to give to the caregivers in the Alzheimer's Unit where Mom had been a patient. "It was a good day, Dad."

"Yes, it was."

Eight years ago, I took Dad two-thirds of the way up Guadalupe Peak. It was a fun father-son day, and I was proud of him for hiking so far at eighty years old, and for knowing when to turn back and hike down. "Dad, this is the first time I've hiked when I was the youngest guy in the group."

Thirty-three years ago, my dad gave me a ride home after my first attempt to run a marathon. I ran about eighteen miles before dropping out. He told me he was proud of me. I was twenty-seven and needed to hear that as much as when I was ten. The truth is, I have never known a moment of life without being certain my dad was proud of me. It is one of God's greatest gifts.

Thirty-eight years ago, I told my Dad that Cyndi and I wanted to get married. "We knew that already. What else is new."

Forty-nine years ago, my dad encouraged me to join the beginner band program at Kermit Junior High School. I'm still a musician today because of him. He served as a church worship leader for years and showed me that music was what grown men did.

Fifty years ago, I was with Dad when we both got busted putting an "It's A Boy" sign in a friend's yard after his wife had their first son. I was embarrassed that we were caught in the act. Dad wasn't. "If it had stayed a secret, it would've been a good prank, but he now has a better story to tell his friends—'Do you know what I caught Deane Simpson doing?'"

Sixty years ago, my Dad enrolled me in the Cradle Roll at our church in Big Spring, Texas. I was only one day old and already a Sunday school member. From my Dad I learned what a long and consistent, quiet and unassuming, happy and joking life with God looked like. I've been trying to live up to that ever since.

◆ ◆ ◆ ◆ ◆

These were my comments on Saturday, April 8, 2017, at the memorial service for my father, Cyrus Deane Simpson:

There are so many things I give my dad credit for—things that have turned out to be fundamental characteristics of my life.

The first thing I learned from him is how to find the joke in any situation. To be funny without hurting other people, and to let the other guys get the punch lines and the big laugh.

Once, when I was just a baby, I had a toy that had a suction cup on one end. One Saturday evening Dad stuck it on his head to play with me. He ended up leading worship in church the next morning with a giant blue bruise on his forehead.

Which illustrates . . . in our family, the joke always came first.

I learned about music. My dad was a church worship leader (back then we called them choir directors; later, music ministers) as far back as I can remember. Not only did I learn to love and play church music, but I also learned from his example that music was something men could do. It was a manly activity, as much as hunting or carpentry. I don't know if I would've picked that up from anyone else.

I learned that being a consistent man of faith for an entire lifetime is a noble and worthy and courageous way to live.

I learned my love for cycling. The childhood stories Dad repeated most often were about bike riding . . . and usually about a disastrous crash of some sort.

Dad loved to ride his bike. He often rode two or three times per day, making five or six laps around Manor Park each time.

He was convinced there was a hill within the neighborhood, and kept trying to get Carroll or me to find him a better GPS for his bike so he could document the elevation change and prove the existence of the hill.

Our last ride together was January 29 at the Cycling Club Friendship Ride. We rode for about an hour, and he kept apologizing for making me ride so slowly and missing the opportunity to ride with the rest of the group. I told him I was a big boy, and I knew what I was getting into when I planned this ride.

I learned how to be a trail guide from my dad. We used to spend a lot of time at the Paisano Encampment near Alpine, and he would often put me in charge of leading a group of adults to see his favorite place, which he called "RA Canyon." It was about an hour hike each way. I was ten years old and leading a dozen adults at a time. I felt good that he trusted me to be the trail guide.

I learned to be a life-hacker, which means to simplify tasks and minimize problems, often by finding a work-around and usually involving lots of improvising.

For example, when we lived in Kermit, everyone was taking their dune buggies to the sand hills. Dad didn't have the money to buy a dune buggy or the skills to build one, but he did drive a black Volkswagen Beetle to work every day.

So, he converted that Volkswagen into a dune buggy by installing wider tires. It really looked funny to see a Volkswagen driving up and down the sand dunes.

He also converted it into a camper. He took all the seats out except the driver's seat and built a platform for sleeping, with access panels to store gear, and he and I spent a week camping around the Gila Wilderness in New Mexico.

The ignition switch quit on the car, so he had a friend install a push button on the dash. Then the starter went out, so Dad had a friend install a lawn mower pulley so we could start it by yanking on a rope. The engine cover wouldn't stay up on its own, so he used a short-handled shovel to prop it up.

Looking back, it seems I would have been embarrassed to have to jump out of the car, prop the engine cover with a shovel, and yank on the rope to start it, but I wasn't. It was fun.

I learned from my dad to make do with what we had and keep moving—no excuses

I learned my early packing skills from my dad. Since we owned a long string of Volkswagens, traveling demanded superior packing skills. I don't remember any specific lessons or rules that my dad handed down to me; guys don't really teach skills that way. Dads expect sons to pick up what they know without having to say any words about it. By absorption.

Later, with my own family, I remember one family trip to Cyndi's grandfather's ranch in northeast New Mexico. Byron, our son, packed everything. It was a work of art. He was so good that when we added a passenger on the way home, he absorbed the additional luggage with no loss of effective space. I was so proud I called Dad to tell him.

Our daughter, Katie, is also an exceptional packer. Her in-laws consider her a packing phenomenon, a packing rainmaker.

Anytime someone says, "How will this all fit?" we step up to the task. We learned that from my dad.

I learned my love of being outside on dirt from my dad.

In fact, we hiked Guadalupe Peak together in 2008 to celebrate his eightieth birthday.

We had a great time together on the trail, telling jokes and making wisecracks and making fun of Uncle James.

We hiked three-and-a-half hours before stopping for lunch. I think we were just around the bend from the wooden bridge.

He said, "I'm having a great day, and I would love to make it to the top and phone my friends from the summit, but I don't want to be foolish about this."

I said, "You know, if a teenager hikes too far and too long and blows all his energy and ends up stumbling home in the dark, it's a funny story. If guys our age (fifty-two and eighty) do the same thing, it's just stupid. It isn't a funny story, it's just stupid. We're supposed to know better."

He said, "Well, we don't want to be stupid."

I learned from my Dad to not give up . . . don't stop . . . until they make you.

Just this last January Dad told me he wanted to go on the First Baptist Men's Ski Trip. He said, "The flyer says the age cutoff is eighteen to ninety, so I have two years left."

He was much more mobile, more nimble, when we signed up. But as the date for the trip approached, I got worried about him and wondered whether I could talk him into staying home.

He said, "Well, if I can't do it, I'll come back inside the lodge." He was determined to give it a try before quitting.

As it turned out . . . the ski trip was overtaken by events. He got sick, and his legs got too weak, and I canceled both of us for the trip.

But I learned a lesson. Don't give up on yourself too soon. Don't assume you can't do something until you know you can't. Keep trying.

I learned what sixty years of love looks like.

When I cleaned out Dad's apartment, I found a significant collection of little ceramic skunks, and some stuffed-animal toy skunks. Way back in the early days of my parents' relationship, Dad gave Mom a ceramic skunk and called her "Stinker." It became a personal connection between them.

But my best view of long-term love was watching Dad take care of my mom during her long bout with Alzheimer's. He often visited her two or three times each day and sat with her for hours at a time.

Thank you for joining us today as we celebrate a timely parting but, most important, a joy-filled life.

◆ ◆ ◆ ◆ ◆

My dad died Friday, March 31, 2017. He was eighty-eight years old. I spent a week packing and moving his apartment. It's the sort of thing all families must do occasionally, one of the final steps in saying goodbye.

All we had to pack from his apartment was the bit of furniture and odds and ends he needed to live, and my dad didn't need much. Most of what was in the apartment was what we moved in for him in 2011, and it was mostly in the same place where we first put it.

Well, except for a significant collection of southern gospel CDs, DVDs, and VHS tapes that his sister, Betty, brought for him to enjoy. I packed at least eight banker's boxes full of those.

We found . . .

Clothes belonging to my mom that had been in the same dresser drawers for at least ten years. Apparently, Dad didn't need the space.

Clothes belonging to Dad, all completely worn out. He wasn't the sort to pay attention to details like clothes, and he only bought more when someone told him to. Except for cycling gear, that is. He had several jerseys and shorts. None of us ever saw him in shorts until about three years ago. Then they became all he wore.

An assortment of magnifying lenses and devices, a variety of hearing aids, all things he added to adjust to the changes in his own body during the past years

A handful of doggie sweaters for his little jumpy dog, Lucy. While his kids were growing up, Dad never allowed dogs in the house; they lived in the backyard. Now, not only did Lucy have free run of the inside, but she had sweaters.

Boxes of notes and records from Dad's twenty years of genealogy research. I found a cousin to take them and make sense of them.

An N-scale train kit that Dad got for Christmas. He was hoping to reboot his hobby of model trains, but his eyesight limited his ability to do detail work more than he anticipated.

Ski clothes laid for the First Baptist Church Men's Ski Trip. He was planning to stay warm. I found six complete pairs of old-school white cotton long underwear in his suitcase, all for a three-day springtime ski trip.

Of course, moving is more than boxing belongings. It's about stories. The stories we tell over and over, the stories we keep in our heart, the stories we cherish to remember people we love, the stories that define us. All those stories are linked to the artifacts we keep around us in our home. So when it comes time to move, it is a process of editing and filtering stories, not just thinning the load. It is never a small thing. It is a nontrivial process.

I was reminded of the days when life treated my mom and dad more gently, before Alzheimer's, when daily living came a little easier. It was a subtle lesson on how two quite different individuals accommodated each other and leaned into each other for fifty-nine years. How they made space for each other in their crowded lives.

Packing up someone else's house is the triage of life—keeping things of value and painfully leaving the rest behind. Not because the past was unimportant but because life is about the future, about grand ideas and bold plans. We must make room for what is still to come.

Chapter 3

Ongoing Hope

One Saturday Cyndi and I rendezvoused with our daughter, Katie, in Abilene, halfway between our house in Midland and Katie's house in Mansfield. Katie handed off her own two daughters, Madden (then age four) and Landry (age one), and what seemed to be three hundred pounds of baby gear. The girls were going to spend a week with their Gran and Pops.

I don't need to go into detail how busy it was for us as we tried to remember how we used to take care of little kids, balancing our time with the girls and our full lives. We were much better thirty years ago; we seemed to have lost our edge, and a few strategic skills, since then.

However, it was great, and we finished the week looking forward to next summer's visit.

Of course, since I went to my office to work during the day, Cyndi spent the most time with the girls. The only time I had them to myself was each evening while she taught yoga classes. Cyndi took them to play with Pattie's two grandsons, to swimming lessons, to the Children's Museum, to the water park in

Andrews, and everywhere else. I'm sure she has more stories and insights than me (but she'll have to write her own account to tell about all that).

Since we had the girls for only one week, we dedicated all our available time and energy to them. I didn't do any of the things I normally did while Cyndi taught her evening classes. No running, biking, or going to the gym. I kept remembering the advice of Dr. Leo Cooney, founder and director of the Section of Geriatrics at the Yale School of Medicine: "If you have to decide between going to the gym or being with your grandchildren, I'd choose the grandchildren."[6]

Done. Thanks, Dr. Cooney.

So instead of all those workouts, it was conversations like these . . .

"Look girls, Gran made us Neelix Rolls, a family favorite"
"Pops, can I have another cinnamon roll?"
"What would your mom say?"
"Well, what do you say?"
"Sure. Here you go."

"Pops, do you know how to skip?"
"Not anymore."

"Pops, can you read this book to me?" (It's a copy of Confessions by St. Augustine)
"Come back in twenty years."

"Here is another sticker for your shirt, Pops. It's a sparkle star."

"Thanks. It looks great on my black polo."

"Hey, Pops, what does a monarch butterfly say?"

"African or European?"

"Do you have Hello Kitty on your phone?"

"Not since Gran made me take it off. She said I was wasting too much time."

"Pops, will you fix my hair?" as we walk into church Sunday morning. I have already brushed it, foolishly thinking that will be enough. Later, when it becomes clear to her I have no idea how to fix her hair the way she imagines it: "Call Gran on your phone so she can come fix my hair."

"Cyndi, do you think it would be OK if I took the girls on a bike ride if they sit in the trailer?"

"No. Landry is only one year old. She's too small; she'll tumble over on her head."

"Besides that part, would it be OK? What if I found a bike helmet?"

"No."

At Chic-fil-A : "Hey Madden, are you big enough to get me a refill?"

"Yes."

"Do you know where to go?"

"To the counter."

"Do you know what I want?"

"Diet Coke."

"Good girl."

While sitting in my lap watching the Tour de France: "When will this race ever be done, Pops?"

"In three weeks."

"That's too long."

"Cyndi, how do you feel about putting a baby on the floor to finish off all the bits of carrots she threw down? Because Landry seems to enjoy her second helping." (I didn't set her on the floor for this specific reason. The girl just loves to be there. She found the food on her own and cleaned it up before I could get to it. Good girl.)

♦ ♦ ♦ ♦ ♦

When I was young, I spent a significant part of each summer at my grandparents' house. I remember my grandmother telling me, "You can't catch a fish if they hear you talking." Silly me, I thought she was giving me fishing advice. She just wanted me to be quiet for a bit. It makes more sense to me now that I'm a grandparent myself.

Here's the thing. A huge spiritual root in my life grew from the time I spent with my grandparents. They invested their lives and faith in me, and I benefit from that still, fifty years later. That sort of impact is what I'm hoping for with the granddaughters in our house.

Babies are stuck with the family they fall into. It is up to us to rise to the occasion, just like my parents and grandparents did, and live lives of honor and grace and gratitude. Holding Madden and Landry was another call to action for me. I'm hoping for lots more opportunities.

♦ ♦ ♦ ♦ ♦

The original plan was to ski at Santa Fe, which we'd done the previous two spring breaks, since Ski Santa Fe has an excellent kid's ski program called Chipmunk Corner. But since New Mexico didn't get enough snow this year, we cobbled together enough Southwest Airlines points to get us all to Salt Lake City, all seven of us: Tonya and Kevin and friend Wade, Cyndi and me, and Madden and Landry.

We stayed in the Brighton Lodge, a ski-in-ski-out place located very near the lifts. Their webpage says it "offers comfortable rustic hotel-style accommodation." It reminded me of a European youth hostel, with small rooms and a shared commons area. All seven of us stayed in our own tiny two-room lodge.

It felt like a college trip, with every flat surface covered by a sleeping person. We had to step over suitcases and around gear and each other to maneuver to the bathroom or front door. The commons area was shared by all the guests, so the first morning both granddaughters, still in their pajamas, ate their cereal while surrounded by a half-dozen men from Argentina. "Your girls are beautiful," they said.

Since we had seven people (including two teenaged boys) and three beds, deciding where we would sleep was our most complicated puzzle. After discussing several options, including making the boys sleep outside, the best solution had me sharing a queen-sized bed with the two girls, eight and four years old, which means I slept on the outside eight inches and the girls tossed around the remaining fifty-two. We were usually so tired after skiing all day that we fell asleep right away, so the beds didn't matter very much anyway.

One night I was reading in bed while trying to quiet the girls when the youngest, Landry, asked, "Pops, are you stuck on a word?" In her preschool no one reads silently, so her only possible explanation for me holding a book without making a sound would be if I were stuck trying to pronounce a word. She offered, "All you have to do is sound out the letters one at a time."

♦ ♦ ♦ ♦ ♦

We were all back in Santa Fe the next year, skiing over the New Year's holidays. Except for six-year-old Landry, that is. She broke her left arm in early December. She told me she fell off her unicorn while galloping around the park. She was still in a cast during our ski trip; Cyndi and I had no qualms about letting her ski anyway since she doesn't use poles and she is so close to the ground, but we knew the ski school would never admit someone in a cast. So her mother, Katie, stayed in town with her the first day, Cyndi stayed with her the second day, and I stayed with her the third day.

Our plan was to drive home to Midland after the third day of skiing, which meant Landry and I packed up all our gear and loaded the pickup and checked out of the hotel before noon. Then we went to the movie, Frozen II, which she had already seen—she knew all the songs and much of the dialogue—then to Chick-fil-A, so I could sit and read and write, and Landry could play in the indoor playground.

She saw me working a Sudoku puzzle and scooted her chair up beside mine. "I'm great at puzzles, Pops. We can do this together."

I explained the rules and we sort of worked together. After about ten minutes she looked at me and said, "Pops, this has been my best day ever."

"But your mom and Gran took you snow sledding on their days in town, and you did lots of other fun stuff. All you and I did was load up the truck and sit in a restaurant."

"Well, Gran is kind of strict, but you aren't."

That's what happens when your Gran is a retired elementary school teacher who doesn't get pushed around easily, but your Pops is an easy mark.

While we were in the restaurant, I ordered a book for Landry, The Super Sudoku Book for Smart Kids, so she could work on some puzzles after she got home.

Later, the next week, I texted her mother: "I had a great time with Landry. I was happy how quickly she grasped the basic rules of Sudoku. But more, at her clever jokes (about going to see Frozen when it was so cold and snowy outside, for example), and her comments during the movie. You were the same way, and I haven't heard that from someone so young since you."

After the book arrived, Landry was happiest about the title, that it was a book for Smart Kids.

♦ ♦ ♦ ♦ ♦

I was sitting on the back porch at a guest house in Angel Fire, New Mexico, reading from my Daily Bible in Isaiah 51:1:

"Listen to me, you who pursue righteousness
and who seek the Lord:
Look to the rock from which you were cut
and to the quarry from which you were hewn."

It's one of my favorite things about reading through the same version of The Daily Bible year after year: passages come at me at the same time of the year and at similar events in my life. Some passages that I might not notice otherwise take on special significance because of the particular day I read them.

I have these notes written in the margin of my Bible, each from a different era of my life:

I was cut from a quarry of Baptist preachers
I am a piece that was cut, that was hewn

As I get older, I want to be the rock itself, the quarry

Maybe I'd rather be the stonecutter.

For several years I've read the very same verses in Isaiah just prior to attending our family reunion.

I liked this notion of "the rock from which you were cut." Isaiah went on to point out Abraham and Sarah, so we know he was referring to people—to ancestors, predecessors, parents and grandparents—when he wrote about "the rock." He reminded those of us who seek the Lord to draw strength from our family.

Sitting in a room with 130-plus members of a family, it is fairly easy to pick out those who married in (like me) and those who are part of the family gene pool. No one can escape the power of genetics or the influence of their raising. I'm sure we'd all like to think we're self-made and independent, but we can't deny the "quarry from which we were hewn." It's written in our faces and our actions.

One thing about quarries: they are seldom homogeneous rock. There are always variations and fractures. Blocks of stone cut from the same quarry are never absolutely identical. They are all a little different.

And so it is with a family quarry. We are not a homogeneous band. We may be alike, but we are also different, with many variations and shades and fractures. We unwittingly pass along some variations or impurities we wish would remain hidden, and we propagate fractures we wish would heal.

At family reunions you often hear the phrase "He's a chip off the old block" to describe how appearance and character are passed down. But I've never heard anyone use it about themselves, as in, "I'm a chip off the old block." Maybe we like ourselves, and maybe we are proud of our lineage, but I doubt anyone wants to be a chip off of anything. We want to be ourselves, not someone else's chip.

However, unlike a block of cut stone, we humans can be choosy about whom we emulate. We can take steps to avoid the fractures. We can be picky about whom we admire. We can choose which blocks to be a chip off of.

A few years ago, when I helped my grandmother write her autobiography and family history, I was reminded how many

Baptist preachers, deacons, church officers, and women's leaders are in my lineage. There is a rich vein of grace and strength that runs through my DNA, and I feel the blessing, even the obligation, that comes with that. It is my provenance, and I hope to live up to it. I want to be a quality rock, a source rock, a rich vein, a deep, long-lasting quarry.

I wrote this in my journal: "I have been blessed because of the faithfulness of my parents and grandparents and great-grandparents. I hope my children are blessed because of my faithfulness. Thank You, Lord, for the strength You have put into my life."

Chapter 4

Love for a Lifetime

Friday morning, Cyndi and I woke up together after two snoozes on the alarm, and we immediately made the bed. It's something we seldom fail to do no matter how busy our morning is. I think we've made the bed every morning since we first got married. We even make the bed when we know our housekeeper will come and change the sheets later in the day. We've been known to do it when staying it in a hotel room. It seems important to maintain the practice.

Occasionally, like last Friday when we get up at the same time, we make the bed together, one on each side of the bed. That is the exception, however. Mostly one of us does it by ourselves, whoever gets out of bed last.

I doubt I ever made my bed when I was a young boy. I don't remember even noticing, much less caring about it. It became a habit for me, and also for Cyndi, when we lived in our dorm rooms in college. All of life happened inside that small, cramped space, and a messed-up bed made the space seem even smaller.

The practical reason we make the bed every morning is because it's so much more pleasant crawling into a made bed at the end of the day than to crawl into a mess of sheets and bedspread.

What are the spiritual reasons for making the bed? It's a small move toward consciously being present, noticing and settling our surroundings. It's one way to take ourselves seriously and an attempt to shape the day by starting it off with structure and aesthetic.

Lately Cyndi and I have adopted a new wrinkle, so to speak, in our habit of bed maintenance. Whichever one of us goes to bed first, before we climb in, we remove the show pillows and turn down the sheets on the other side to make it easier for the other person. It's a welcoming gesture. And if Cyndi crawls into bed first, she usually also turns on my reading light.

In his book Soul Salsa, Leonard Sweet wrote about the rituals of our lives that help us "grow our own souls by modulating the mundane into the eternal."[7]

I showed that quote to Cyndi and asked if she thought we had any rituals. Making the bed was the first thing that occurred to her. We probably had more rituals back when Byron and Katie were younger and lived at home with us. We certainly had a more predictable routine. Nowadays our rituals are mostly about taking care of each other.

Besides making the bed, we thought about this: when either of us leaves the house, we don't just yell goodbye or leave and expect the other person to know. We find each other and kiss goodbye, even if only making a quick errand run to the grocery store. Maybe one reason is because we are fully aware of the dangers in our world and how something sudden and fatal could happen to either of us, so we want to at least have a last kiss.

But I doubt this is the main reason; we aren't that fearful or fatalistic. I think it has more to do with acknowledging the importance of each of us in the other's life, of recognizing existence, of saying, "Yes, I see you."

Or it could be we just like kissing.

I don't know if the following is a ritual, but I'm crediting it as one: I won't—that is to say, I can't—walk past Cyndi, whether in a crowded hallway or an open room, at home or at Rosa's or at church, without brushing against her, dragging my hand across her back or her bottom. I try to be subtle, and I doubt many outsiders notice it, but I do it every time. Why? I'm touching base, tagging up, reminding her I'm close and, even more, that I notice her. I'm saying: I see you, and I'm drawn to you, and I'm still hot for you.

Here's another: we eat at least 99 percent of our home meals in the kitchen, with no distracting TV, even if we're just eating a quick sandwich. Only occasionally will we eat in front of a movie, or a ballgame, or our laptops; a dozen times a year at most. I'll admit that some of you who know us are shaking your head and wondering: When are you at home and not eating at Rosa's or Jason's. That would be an accurate observation. I don't think we have any rituals for restaurants.

However, I would add that Cyndi and I pray before meals, whether in public or at home, a practice both of us learned from our families, and it is definitely a sacred ritual. It's a pause to recognize God as Lord of our lives and giver of all things, and to acknowledge we have been blessed.

Sometimes when we are eating with other people who don't have the same praying ritual, we will look at each other and let it pass. It isn't our desire to make our companions feel awkward or uncomfortable. But just last week we were having dinner with a friend in San Angelo and she wouldn't let us pass. She said, "Oh, you two always like to ask a blessing for the food, don't you," as she grabbed our hands.

Sweet wrote, "The challenge of discipleship is to make one's own life a sacrament, a sign of love and grace, a sacred gesture inserted in a world flaunting other gestures."[8] I believe our small gestures are indeed spiritual practices, disciplines we stick to so our hearts stay soft toward each other and toward God.

♦ ♦ ♦ ♦ ♦

According to the version of the story that Cyndi tells, she didn't know all that much about what our Thursday evening consisted of either, but I knew, when I saw her in that short turquoise dress with her cowboy boots, that she was planning to have fun.

Earlier in the week she'd told me the Perrys had invited us to join them at their table for a fundraising dinner. Of course, we said yes. We've never been anywhere or done anything with them that didn't turn out to be great fun.

All I knew was that we were having dinner together, and there would probably be some form of entertainment or speaker. This lack of information was unusual because I'm typically the one of the two of us who checks all the details beforehand. Not this time.

It turned out to be an outside dinner with gourmet tacos and roasted ears of corn. Perfect. I couldn't have been happier. Until, that is, I looked up at the stage and saw the huge sign behind all the sound equipment that read Los Lonely Boys.

"Are you kidding me?" I asked Cyndi. "The Los Lonely Boys are playing tonight? I thought it was some local cultural arts folk group."

Cyndi shrugged and said, "I guess so. I didn't know, either."

About two songs into the Los Lonely Boys' first set, I knew it was time to ask Cyndi to dance. Well, she actually broached the topic before I did, but I knew it was imminent when she started swaying in her chair and smiling, so I had my answer ready. There was a time in my life—say, my first fifty years—when I never would've gotten up in front of an entire dinner-and-concert crowd to dance near the stage. That is, unless sixty or seventy couples started dancing first. This was mostly because I had no confidence dancing, fueled by the fact I had no skills, either. I only have about two moves, and they both involve the two-step.

On the other hand, when Cyndi dances, her entire body lights up. There is a glow of energy surrounding her. Even her shoulders smile. How can I possibly not be part of that?

She lured me in close with her sparkling eyes, not that I had any plans to resist, and before I knew what had happened, we were dancing alone near the stage, the very first couple to give it a whirl. All by ourselves.

After a couple minutes of being the only people dancing at all, Cyndi smiled and said, "I love you, Berry."

"I know. And so does everyone else who can see us. It's no secret anymore."

Eventually the Perrys joined our dancing for a part of the song, but they were the only ones all night. I didn't mind. I was so infatuated by my date and overwhelmed by how great our evening turned out that I was sparkling just like Cyndi.

♦ ♦ ♦ ♦ ♦

Paul Simon's tune "Fifty Ways to Leave Your Lover" was a fun song back in 1975, but it didn't describe the life I was interested in. I preferred Dan Fogelberg's song from 1982, "Make Love Stay."

Love has done so. July 28, 2019, marked forty years of marriage for Cyndi and me. In 1979 when we got married, Cyndi was twenty-one and I was twenty-three; that seemed older then than it does now.

We ask each other all the time, why have we stayed married for so long when others don't? We aren't so arrogant as to think it has all been up to us, though we've certainly worked hard at our relationship. We've seen too many other perfect marriages fall apart, often couples we knew well. The truth is, to each of us, no other life looks better, or more exciting or fulfilling, than staying married to each other. Our love grows deeper and richer year by year, and I can't wait to see what it looks like in 2059 for our eightieth.

I made a list of some of the things that have worked for us. They're randomly sorted because I'm not smart enough to rank them. Of course, this is only a partial list. My first draft had sixty items. Playing off of Neil Simon's tune, here are . . .

Forty Ways to Keep Your Lover

1. Be proud and brag. Boast about your spouse's accomplishments in public and let them overhear your boasting.
2. Don't complain. Never complain about each other to someone else. I don't complain to my family or friends about Cyndi, and she doesn't complain about me to hers. It's hard

to say, "I'm sorry, I was wrong," once the group battle lines have been drawn.
3. Trust each other. It isn't easy for any of us to ask for help. Be vulnerable and ask.
4. Be loyal. Cyndi and I see ourselves as a two-member team, back-to-back against all boarders.
5. Grace. Don't say, "I told you so." There is nothing to gain from that except to feel like you're the hero and your spouse is the loser.
6. Flirt. Never stop flirting with each other—serious, frequent, grown-up flirting. She has often asked me, when in a store trying on clothes, "Come in the dressing room and feel me in this."
7. New. Read to each other from new books and share new things you just learned.
8. Listen. Intentionally listen to each other. Cyndi will sit and listen to me read on and on from my journal, especially after I come down from a solo backpacking trip. It's a rare gift.
9. Dancing. I've learned the courage to dance with Cyndi, and she has the grace and patience to dance with me.
10. Together. You don't have to do everything together; however, we climb mountains, go to yoga class, ride bikes, enjoy study dates at Rosa's, play music, run races and marathons, and hold hands whenever anyone is praying.
11. Guard. Jealously guard those few opportunities to be close. Back in the day, we never let the kids sit between us at church. That was our space.
12. Share. Let your spouse safely share their weirdest ideas, rawest thoughts, and edgiest philosophies.

13. Space. Some of the best advice given to us before we married was to find our individual lives apart from each other. It seemed crazy at the time since being apart from each other was what we were trying to eliminate, but we learned to give each other space. We don't have to do everything together.
14. Learn. Take every personality test or compatibility survey you find. Learn more about each other, how to take care of each other, and respond to each other. Through the years, Cyndi and I have learned to enjoy our differences as an asset.
15. Money. Don't fall into the trap of "my money vs. your money." We've always treated money as "ours," no matter whose bank account it sat in. And yet, one of my favorite gifts was when Cyndi bought my road bike. The checkbook she used had both our names on it, but she made a point of writing and signing the check, endorsing my new adventure. I told everyone I knew.
16. Always changing. Allow each other room to change through the years. No one stays married to just one person, even if we marry only one person. We all change and grow.
17. Impression. Make it a point to never appear like you're looking around for a better deal. Not even a hint.
18. PDA. There's nothing wrong with some public display of affection. Cyndi and I have even been busted in the church hallway. I remember one time at home when one of our teenagers saw us kissing and told us to "get a room." I pointed out, "These are all our rooms."
19. Support. Support each other's adventures, whether running marathons, playing trombone and congas, buying a yoga studio, or hiking the Colorado Trail.

20. Music. Reinforce those deep bonds that first brought you together. Cyndi and I first met in a high school band hall in 1973 and fell for each other at a One O'clock Jazz Band concert in 1976. We've played together in the First Baptist Church orchestra since the late 1980s and have recently traveled on music mission trips together to Israel, Guatemala, and Hungary.
21. Simple decisions. Work out a system for making those decisions that drive couples crazy, as in, where to eat or what to watch. For us, the first person makes three to five suggestions, and the second must pick from that list. We both end up satisfied.
22. Abandon. Give up the notion that your spouse will make you feel completely satisfied all the time.
23. Show up. Show up for each other every day.
24. Assume good intentions. Give your partner the benefit of the doubt in all conversations and decisions.
25. Side by side. Cyndi held me and believed in me when I got laid off . . . four times.
26. Origin Story. Talk often of your early days, how you found each other, why you fell in love.
27. Faith. Our shared faith is one of the first things that drew us together. Through the years, our best conversations have been about faith and theology and ministry, and some of our best times together have been worshiping and ministering.
28. Attractive. Do the hard work required to stay attractive for each other. Don't leave any opening for buyer's remorse.
29. Friends. Surround yourself with people who support your marriage. Avoid negative people and negative situations.

30. Chores. Take time to make the bed or carry out the trash, even though you know if you don't the other one probably will. Small gestures of tact and consideration add up.
31. Advice. Be careful. Unsolicited advice always feels like criticism regardless of your intentions.
32. Songs. Play love songs for each other often. Let them soften your heart like they did in the beginning.
33. Lucky. Know that each of you is the lucky one.
34. Hands. Lots of handholding, especially when driving down the highway.
35. Never assume. Don't take your relationship for granted just because you're married. Courting and winning each other's heart and attention is a lifelong adventure.
36. Friends. Meet each other's friends and coworkers. I assume no one knows me well until they know Cyndi too.
37. Your song. Whatever *your song* is, respond to it. Anytime I hear the song *Fallen*, by Lauren Wood, I know Cyndi is moving toward me with arms outstretched, ready to dance.
38. Rescue. Protect each other from long (or bad) conversations with crazy people. Cyndi was especially good at this back in my government days.
39. Attention. Notice when your spouse enters a room full of people. Cyndi often walks across a crowded room simply to stand next to me within arm's reach. I always take advantage and pull her in closer.
40. Decide. Make the decision to be in your marriage for the distance. No detours, no turning back, no dropping out, no cutting the course.

♦ ♦ ♦ ♦ ♦

Somewhere out of Jonesborough, Tennessee, Cyndi and I ended up on the wrong highway. We don't know how or where we went wrong, except to claim there were no landmarks to catch and hold our attention. All we could see while driving were miles and miles of trees and mountains, a confusing scene to desert-dwelling flatlanders like us.

We were in Tennessee for the National Storytelling Festival, which we enjoyed immensely but had to leave early and fly back to Midland Saturday afternoon because we needed to do some adulting (isn't that what the kids are saying nowadays?)

We stayed at the festival as long as we could, until noon, listening to Bill Lepp describe how he creates stories. Then we dashed off to our rental car (which was actually a manager's-special minivan), hoping to make the Charlotte airport in time for our 4:25 departure.

According to the highway signs, we passed several towns, but all we ever saw were trees and mountains. In West Texas we put our towns out in plain view to show them off, but these Appalachians tuck their towns behind tall, green obstacles.

As we neared the airport, we stopped to fill up our rental car with gasoline before returning it. Cyndi had her credit card in her left hand and the door handle in her right hand as I pulled beside the pump. By the time I turned off the engine, she had jumped out, dashed around to the driver's side, grabbed the nozzle, and was entering our zip code in the keypad. I removed the gas cap and she filled the tank. We were back on the road in less than one minute. We weren't late yet.

We made it through the airport maze and found Rental Car Return on our first pass, literally a good sign. As we screeched into the return lane, leaping out of the car like a SWAT team, Cyndi told the attendant we were racing to catch our flight, so the young woman typed madly into the hand-held computer and called out as we took off, "I'll email your receipt."

I had my boarding pass on my phone thanks to my Southwest Airlines app, but I couldn't pull up Cyndi's pass, and neither could Cyndi. That meant I could go straight through security, but she had to have her pass printed at the check-in counter.

Cyndi wanted me not to wait for her but go on to the gate, but I didn't want to do that. What if she got hung up and didn't make the flight? I said, "I'm not going anywhere without you."

Cyndi maneuvered her way through the check-in switchbacks, slinking and stretching like an experienced yoga teacher, to an unused kiosk. Looking over her shoulder she suggested again that I go to the gate. "Tell them I'm coming, so maybe they'll hold the plane."

I've been around long enough to know not say no twice, so I took off. I made it through TSA precheck quickly except for when they had to dial up the body scanner just for me since my aftermarket knees set off the standard metal detector.

It turned out to be a long, long way from TSA to the departure gate. Even worse, the Charlotte airport, while delightful in every other way, has mind-numbingly slow moving sidewalks. They are so slow you might fall over if you stood still. Fortunately, I was running and not walking, so my balance was fine.

I tumbled into Gate A3 just as the last people in line were boarding, and before I asked them to wait for Cyndi, I looked back down the long hallway and saw her running toward me. She was beautiful, and smiling, and knew, finally, she would make the flight home. Our reunion was like one of those videos where two lovers run toward each other in a flower-filled meadow, arms outstretched, music playing—only we weren't in slow motion and I had my foot stuck in the entrance to the jetway like a door-to-door encyclopedia salesman keeping it open.

We made it.

As we slid into two adjoining seats, I remembered how one of the storytellers, Jerron Paxton, told a joke about using a dating app on his phone. When no one laughed, he looked out across the room of gray-headed and white-headed couples and said, "I guess you folks don't have a need for a dating app." And then he added, "You seem pretty settled."

Part Two

Living an AUTHENTIC Life

Chapter 5

Growing through Failure

There are surprising advantages to growing older; each year is a slightly higher platform for viewing the past. I was thinking about that when I heard a podcast speaker ask, "What would you attempt if you knew you couldn't fail?" He was implying that the fear of failure was stopping us from attempting what we truly wanted.

By the time I arrived at my favorite writing booth in Whataburger, the question had morphed into this: How has personal failure changed me and shaped our family's life?

Of course, I started making a list.

What Would Have Been Different If I'd Gone through Life Never Failing

- I would be braver if I knew I couldn't fail, but without the risk of failure what is the meaning of courage?
- I would never have learned humility from having to start over so often after losing my job so many times.

- I would believe our family's destiny, safety, and success depended solely on my economic decisions and brain power.
- I would've never experienced the restless heart that's pulled me toward God.
- I would've succeeded in my first attempt at the Golden Yucca Marathon, never fully appreciating how difficult it was.
- I wouldn't have needed all those time-consuming and often painful training runs before each marathon. I could've simply lined up and run without preparation—and missed the deep spiritual meditations that came from those advance runs.
- I would still have the same misguided belief of self-sufficiency and invulnerability I had when I was twenty.
- I would've never experienced the strengthening, maturing, and seasoning that comes from a failure-laden journey.
- I wouldn't have sought out sages for wisdom and advice. I would still think success was all about me.
- I would have no patience with those who are suffering and those who fail.
- I would have leaped up the corporate ladder moving to California, missing so many ministries and relationships in Midland.
- I wouldn't know what it means to prepare.
- I would've jumped into teaching opportunities way too soon, before I found my voice or, more importantly, before I found my life message.
- I would never have needed, understood, or experienced forgiveness.
- I wouldn't have learned to listen to advice.

- I would be worthless to anyone asking my advice, since failure is the only way we really learn anything worthy of sharing.
- I would've never learned to give credit to others.
- I would've never learned to recognize bad advice.
- I would've never learned the details of why success happens.
- I would not understand or know risk. And without risk, there is no room for love, only conquest.
- I would never have learned that Plan B is often better than Plan A.
- I would've never learned how to learn.
- I would've never known anyone smarter than me
- I would've never learned the joy of spontaneous improvisation in sticky situations.
- I would've never known how much I needed grace and never learned how to give grace away.

We love to quote the movie Apollo 13: "Failure is not an option."[9] But the statement is wrong. Failure is not only a live option, but also a certainty. If the oxygen tank in the Apollo 13 service module hadn't failed, turning a moon landing into a rescue mission, NASA would never have had their "finest moment."

◆ ◆ ◆ ◆ ◆

When Cyndi and I got married, I'm sure I was not ready (since I had no idea what "ready" meant), but I spent a lot of time preparing. I probably *thought* I was ready.

Then we had our first child, Byron. We were neither prepared nor ready. God blessed us with a sweet baby boy before we had a clue, and we had to learn on the fly. Had we waited until we were ready, it's possible we'd still be waiting.

For my first marathon attempt, I thought I was prepared and ready, but the race showed me I wasn't. I came back a year later with essentially the same training and fitness but with a greater respect for the distance and demands, and I was successful.

When I made my first solo backpacking trip into the Guadalupes, I was neither prepared nor ready. I had inadequate gear and scant knowledge, but I went anyway because I was tired of my own excuses.

As a writer, it took me way too long to finally publish my first book. I never thought I was ready. Now, working on my fifth, I realize I will never be fully prepared, and I'll have to keep learning what I need to know through the writing process itself.

Ultramarathon runner Dean Karnazes wrote about his first attempt at the Western States 100 and his run up the summit of Emigrant Pass and the peak of Granite Chief, at 9,050 feet elevation. As he neared the top, he found himself in a short line of runners waiting to get water at the aid station. He was in the classic runner's position, bent over at the waist with hands on knees gasping for breath. One of the aid workers filled Dean's water bottles and then said, "You're not going to be able to catch your breath standing here, no matter how long you stay. We're too high up in the sky."[10] His only hope was to keep moving.

It's important to know that sometimes we will never catch our breath, never catch up, never settle down, and our heart will always be racing. We will never be prepared enough for the next part of the journey. Our best option is to keep moving forward. Keep our legs moving.

The reason I am writing about this is because it's bigger than mountain climbing or marathon running. How many ministry opportunities have we squandered because we didn't think we were ready? How many people failed to get the help they needed because we weren't finished preparing? How many times have we failed to follow God's will claiming the sorry excuse that we aren't ready yet?

Seth Godin asked the question, "I wonder if there's also a moral obligation to start?" He continued, "I believe that if you've got the platform and the ability to make a difference, then this goes beyond 'should' and reaches the level of 'must.' You must make a difference, or you squander the opportunity. Wasting the opportunity both degrades your own ability to contribute and, more urgently, takes something away from the rest of us. To do less is to steal from them."[11]

Moving forward while feeling unready and ill prepared can be scary, I know. But we should be more afraid of lifelong regrets than temporary uncertainty. A life without fear is a life without accomplishment. Cyndi likes to remind me, "Do something brave every day." That usually means being scared and not being ready. If we have the means and ability and passion, we are stealing if we don't act.

♦ ♦ ♦ ♦ ♦

One Monday I was preparing to leave town for a men's retreat in the Rocky Mountains near Colorado Springs, one of the highlights of my year, and getting ready to give a talk while there, an even bigger highlight of my year. My wife got a phone call from someone she followed and respected, a mentor and teacher, who proceeded to dump all over her, call her a liar and such.

When Cyndi told me the story, I was livid. Incensed. Instantly I began sharpening my knives and strapping on ammunition belts. In a corporate setting the man would've been fired, then sued. No one in a position of leadership has a right to talk to anyone like that—only this wasn't just anyone he was talking to; he was talking to my girl, my wife, and I took it personally.

Except that I couldn't really do anything about it other than make a simple complaint since he had it in his power to retaliate against Cyndi. She would suffer from my actions, not me.

I was so angry that it took me too long before I could think about anything else, whether I was awake or asleep. Finally, out of desperation, to settle my heart, I spent Tuesday afternoon listening to one song over and over, a song from 1998 by the band Far From Home titled "I Want to Be Like You." I needed a new heart and a new mind. I needed a mended soul. I was suffering and needed a new start. I knew that if I continued to wallow in my anger, I might never get out.

The song worked; it calmed me down.

By Tuesday night I could sleep. By Wednesday I could make final modifications on my talk. By Thursday I could travel to Colorado and enjoy the retreat. Why? Because God changed my heart.

But I was still a bit angry at the phone caller and knew it would be better if I didn't see him or talk to him for a while, maybe a long while. I didn't want to get into a fight and have Cyndi suffer the consequences. I was still defending Cyndi in my mind and enjoying my own righteousness for being the noble one in the scenario.

And then, after I returned home from the retreat, I learned I'd probably lost one of my best friends because of something I said about his wife. It was a year before at one of our regular lunches. I was surprised that we didn't get back together during the year; now I knew why. I don't remember what I said, and whatever it was, it isn't how I feel. I love her and think the highest of her.

But that doesn't matter. I'm a grown-up and responsible for what I say. Too often I make jokes and wisecracks and don't think about how they come across. Too often I make what I intend as an analytical comment, impersonal, that comes across instead as judgmental and mean. I'm old enough to know better, to be better.

Not only that, but I'm also a teacher and communicator. A good one. Which is all the more reason to be responsible and accountable for everything I say. It isn't enough to have good intentions if I waste them in the way I talk.

And then it occurred to me, in one breathtakingly honest moment, that I was the same as the man who phoned Cyndi. I was the same guy I was so mad at. I was the man who hurt someone who trusted me, because of what I said.

It broke my heart. Who did I think I was? Certainly, no one special, or righteous, or immune from making life-changing mistakes.

I don't know if my friendship will recover, and I don't blame my friend one bit if it doesn't. I hope we can restore what we've lost, but I know it's seldom that easy. Deep damage to the heart aches for a long time. My life will be poorer and smaller without this friendship.

Why am I writing about this? Because in much of my writing, in most of my stories, I end up the hero. That isn't a fair representation of real life. Too often, in reality, I'm the goat.

I'm writing about this because it matters how we live. It matters what we say. It matters how we say it.

We have it in our power to build up or tear down. We can ruin a friendship that was once strong and influential, or we can live a life that lasts a thousand generations. We make those choices every day.

You, therefore, have no excuse, you who pass judgment on someone else, for at whatever point you judge another, you are condemning yourself, because you who pass judgment do the same things. (Romans 2:1)

It was a hard lesson to learn. My anger at someone else condemned me. I don't believe either relationship will be mended soon; maybe never. Losing my friend will leave a scar, but it will be a long reminder to be more careful about what I say. That story of failure isn't the story I want to live. But failure is an inevitable part of risk, and risk is a part of growth, and growth is about succeeding at life, loving more deeply, living more authentically, and being conformed to the image of Jesus.

Chapter 6

Living with New Knees

I had to learn how to walk all over again at age fifty-nine. Well, not completely from scratch. I could still move down the sidewalk on both feet with very little conscious thought, but I still had a hobble in my step, a limp. I still walked like a combination of Granny Clampett from *The Beverly Hillbillies* and Uncle Joe Carson from *Petticoat Junction*. I still walked like I did before having my knees replaced, when they ached with every step.

My knee problems began in 2004, which means I had an entrenched eleven-year muscle memory for walking with a limp, for walking without bending my knees, for hobbling from side to side.

I'm writing about this because recently I noticed myself limping down the hallway in my office, not from surgery but from habit. I wasn't happy to have a persistent limp I didn't need and didn't want. I was capable of walking straight and painlessly, yet there I was, compensating for a condition that no longer existed.

Is it possible to live so long in injury that our bodies forget how to live without it? Is it possible to forget how good life can be? Or do we learn to enjoy limping? After all, it provides a convenient excuse to explain away poor performances.

I know this much: it's possible to limp so long that we make agreements with ourselves. As in, "Pain-free walking just isn't for me," or "I'm stuck in this lousy relationship but I'm used to it now," or "I'm saddled with this addiction for the rest of my life; I should just get used to it."

In her book *I Was Told There'd Be Cake,* Sloane Crosley wrote of the time she was misdiagnosed as having hemochromatosis, a too-much-iron-in-the-blood disease. Later, when she found out she wasn't sick after all, she was a little sad. "I had myself an explanation for everything that had ever been wrong with me," she wrote. "I wanted to hold my flaws close but controlled like a balloon tied to my wrist with a string. If anything went wrong, all I had to do was tug at the string and bring my explanation down for others to see. This is who I am and this is why."[12]

The question we have to ask is this: Do I want to get well?

Jesus asked this same question of a man who had been paralyzed for thirty-eight years. Jesus found him lying by a pool of water, a place where blind, lame, and paralyzed people were left for the day by their families. There was a tradition that when the water was stirred, the first person into the pool was healed. (See John 5:1–9)

Jesus asked the man, "Do you want to get well?"

The man said, "Sir, I have no one to put me in the pool when the water is stirred up, and someone else always steps down ahead of me."

Curiously, the man didn't answer Jesus's question. Instead, he started making excuses. Jesus didn't ask him, "What are your problems? What makes your life so hard?" He asked, "Do you want to get well?" But this man had been sick so long that he forgot about wanting to get well. All he could do was explain his limp.

Too often we settle when we don't have to because we forget how good life can be. We forget about God's healing. We hide behind our limp to avoid living the life God has for us.

♦ ♦ ♦ ♦ ♦

Getting new knees in 2015 was a wakeup alarm for me. I got a new chance to do things, reengage with hiking and running and all that; but also, and more importantly, I understood that I was mortal, my time was limited, and I would eventually age out of everything I love to do.

I'd always wanted to run an ultramarathon on a mountain trail, but I wasted the years when my knees were good. I thought those years would last forever, and I would have plenty of time. I'd get around to running that trail once I was skinny enough and trained up enough. I also put it off because I was afraid of Cyndi's reaction, that she would think I couldn't do it. Then my knees got bad, and I realized that skinny was no longer the issue, and Cyndi's opinion was no longer the issue. My knees were the issue. I was done for.

So this second chance was a reminder that I would not keep getting more chances, and whatever I dreamed of doing I should do now. I was waking up to my life.

♦ ♦ ♦ ♦ ♦

Some things we do because we love them and can't imagine life any other way (writing, backpacking, music, running). Other things we do to develop particular skills (cycling, shooting). Still others we do because they're good for us (weightlifting, taking vitamins). And finally, there are things we do for the person we love (yoga)—oh, and (branding cattle).

Cyndi and I once spent a weekend branding calves. We were near Des Moines, New Mexico, firmly in the Great Plains, in the shadow of two ancient volcanos, Sierra Grande and Capulin.

It's stunning country. The dominant view is infinite grassland and open skies. Looking north, you see nothing standing between you and the Arctic Circle except the curvature of the earth. This is country where all things are open and laid bare, where you can critique a misplaced fence line for miles while standing in one place.

Cyndi and her three cousins started this cattle-raising venture and have referred to it as the Four Chicks Ranch. Since one cousin doesn't want anyone calling her a chick, I suggested Three Chicks and a Hen. She didn't like that name, either.

During the branding operation it was my job to pin the calf down from the front by pushing on its neck with my right knee and pulling up on the top front leg, while my cousin-in-law Bob grabbed both rear legs and pulled outward. We held the calf on the ground while it was tagged, vaccinated, branded, and castrated, hoping no one got kicked in the process. It was my first time to use these new knees for something besides walking, hiking, or cycling, and it all went better than I expected. I could even walk normally the next morning.

Maybe the reason my knees performed so well was I didn't have to think about it. Once a calf was roped, everything occurred too fast. There was no time to consider whether I should jump up or down. No time for trepidation. Is it possible I've babied my knees too much during the months of rehab? Could I have been doing more all this time?

I assumed the reason I was assigned the head of the calf was because the job depended more on body mass than skill level. I changed my mind after watching the real cowboys. Even Kelly, Cyndi's cousin, a young mother of two, flipped calves better than I, and I outweigh her by one hundred pounds.

I'm not sure where learning to flank calves fit into my life plan and One Hundred Life Goals and all that, but I told Cyndi I would add branding to my list so I could check it off.

"Was it on your list before today?"

"Oh no, of course not, I never considered it, but I'm taking credit for it now."

Chapter 7

Moving My Feet

One Saturday afternoon I ran on the Winsor Trail in the Santa Fe National Forest. If you'd seen me, you'd have said I wasn't running at all but walking or, at best, power hiking. Yet it was my best mountain trail run in thirteen years, since Boot Camp at Frontier Ranch near Buena Vista, Colorado, October 2003. It was also my first attempt at trail running since getting my new aftermarket knees twelve months prior, in July 2015. It was a delightful and happy occasion. It felt like the future. It felt like a comeback. Like restoration.

The trail begins at 7,200 feet in Tesuque, New Mexico, just northwest of Santa Fe, and climbs twenty-two miles to the Santa Fe Ski Basin. The upper trailhead is the most popular, but knowing I was going to do a forty-five-minute out-and-back, I wanted my second half to be downhill, so I started at the bottom.

While I was on the trail, I listened to Erwin McManus preach about the Ethiopian eunuch, a man whose entire adult life was defined by what he wasn't, what he couldn't do, and who he couldn't be. That is, until he found a new life and a new definition. The story felt familiar and personal as I hopped over rocks and crossed streams. New hope is an amazing thing.

When people ask how my new knees are doing a year after replacement, I tell them I've started to hope again. I'm dreaming of long hikes, bike rides, runs, things I had given up on.

Mark Rowlands, author of Running with the Pack, wrote, "Any worthwhile achievement changes you in a way that makes what you achieve no longer important to you."[13]

Running has certainly changed me. It led to cycling, weightlifting, and backpacking. You would've suspected none of that if you'd known me in high school. I was the furthest from an athlete you might imagine.

Again, from Rowlands: "Achievement is a process of making the things I achieve not matter anymore. I run not to achieve anything—not in the sense of acquiring something—but to be changed by the process of achieving. I run because I want to be changed."[14]

I can absolutely see that in my life. I have never been a competitive athlete—either in temperament or talent—but I entered races, especially marathons, knowing I would be a changed man afterwards. I have a deep desire to keep changing who I am even as I know I am a man of routine and predictable behavior.

And now, as I ease back into running after getting new knees, I long to do more. I have nothing to prove, and no one cares whether I do it, but I want the process of training long and the discipline of finishing to once again work me over and reshape me. I don't know any other way to accomplish that.

Well, the next day after my run, my feet were stiff and sore. No surprise there since I'd doubled the amount of running time I was used to. The uneven ground and sudden stop-and-starts typical of trail running also made my quads and knees ache. But that unpredictability is why it was so much fun. I was proud of my soreness.

I couldn't have even started a trail run without my renewed hope in the future, but hope is not enough. Sunday's soreness was a reminder that I needed more miles, more training, and more trail experience, to make this work. Hope has to be acted on. We have to live it out. We have to put in miles and training for hope to become reality.

♦ ♦ ♦ ♦ ♦

Last Sunday morning I skipped church and drove to the lake. Not to fish but to run. I parked in one of the lots on the west side of White Rock Lake in Dallas, about halfway between the north and south ends, and assembled my gear. I was running the lake by myself this time; Cyndi was attending a weekend yoga workshop.

Circling a lake is a commitment. There are no shortcuts home. You have to run all the way around, no matter how tired you might be. And this trail is nine miles around. I knew I'd be stiff, sore, and thirsty by the time I got back to the car, so I had my Advil and a large drink ready. After all, I was increasing my regular distance by 200 percent.

My first time to run at White Rock Lake was in December 1985, during my attempt at the Dallas White Rock Marathon. Sadly, I dropped out of the race at mile fifteen due to plantar fasciitis in my right foot. I returned in December 1987 with a vanload of friends, and we all completed the marathon together. It was my second marathon finish and still stands as my personal best time.

In February 1998, when Cyndi and I visited Dallas to celebrate her fortieth birthday, we awoke at 7:00 a.m. and drove to White Rock Lake for a morning nine-miler. The trail was full of people just like us, wearing clothes just like us. It was invigorating to be around so many other distance runners. The energy in the air was contagious. Later, after the adrenaline wore down and the sweat stopped dripping, Cyndi and I drove to La Madeleine for a low-impact breakfast in front of the fireplace. After that day, we planned all our Dallas trips around finding time to run at the lake. Of course, Cyndi always ran off and left me, but since we drove to and from the lake in the same car, it seemed like we were doing it together. Those mornings are some of our favorite stories.

This run last Sunday, on the final weekend of April, was something I'd been planning for weeks. I was celebrating a big anniversary. Forty years ago, in May 1978, I started running. I had just completed my first senior year at the University of Oklahoma when I returned home to Hobbs, New Mexico, to work as a summer engineer for Getty Oil Company. Within my first week I realized my plans for the summer were in trouble: the girl I'd dated the previous summer, who attended New Mexico Junior College and whom I hoped to date again, had been seeing a track-and-field jock during the school year. A javelin thrower, of all people. How could I compete for her attention against a guy like that? I needed something besides good grades in college to win her back.

After analyzing my dilemma, I did something uncharacteristic for me—something that shaped the rest of my life. I decided to run. If I intended to compete with a jock for the affections of Cyndi Richardson, I had to do something physical, and running was the easiest thing I could think of. It was the first voluntary run of my life. In fact, other than an occasional touch football game or church softball game, it was my first voluntary attempt at any sport besides ping-pong.

I ran almost every day that summer in Stan Smith Adidas tennis shoes (a big mistake) and Levi cutoffs (an even bigger mistake). Eventually, after beating my knees and chafing my legs, I realized the importance of buying real running shoes and better shorts.

My campaign to win Cyndi's heart proved successful in spite of my marginal performance as an athlete. I suppose it was my charm that she fell in love with. (She says it was my eyes that worked, the way I looked at her.) By August I was enjoying my daily runs, so I kept it up when I went back to school. And surprisingly, I stuck to it; I ran four or five times a week that entire school year.

Once I started running, I never stopped. I've spent hundreds of hours running, and to my surprise, all that time on my feet became a private meditation. It was the catalyst that moved me toward a deeply personal, contemplative faith that strengthens my life even today. Almost every spiritual insight I've had has happened while moving my feet down the road. I've gone out running dozens of times with the specific intent to hear from God about an upcoming decision or particularly sticky relationship, and he has spoken to me time and time again during those miles.

After Cyndi and I married I continued to run, mostly every day. And then, for some reason, I joined the West Texas Running Club. And that led to my signing up for my first race, a five- and ten-miler in Lubbock in the summer of 1980.

I also don't know why the marathon song started playing in my head, but I was reading Runner's World magazine, I discovered George Sheehan's books, and the next thing I knew, I had signed up to run the Golden Yucca Marathon in Hobbs in November 1981. I had to drop out after mile sixteen, most likely because I had no idea how to train, but I came back again in 1983 to run the entire marathon.

Running became part of my public identity, how I thought of myself, what I did all the time in all kinds of weather, even on business trips and vacations. It was physically, emotionally, and spiritually satisfying.

Because Cyndi I both enjoyed running, it became a lifelong adventure for us. We try to work in a run wherever we go. We've run in Hawaii, Kenya, Denmark, Singapore, China, Budapest, and near the Sea of Galilee in Israel.

Running provided my first opportunity to write stories for other people to read in The Rundown, our club newsletter. From that beginning, I've published a weekly blog since 1998, and four books (so far).

Running also led to my love of parks and trails, which landed me on the Midland Parks and Recreation Board, and eventually to twelve years of elected service on the city council.

Never in my wildest imagination did I anticipate that daily running would become instrumental in how I lived my life, how I planned my time, where I traveled for fun and leisure, how I met my friends, and how I ended up serving in local government. The daily dose of being alone on my feet became an integral part of my next forty years. In fact, those nine miles around White Rock Lake last Sunday morning pushed my lifetime total to 37,495 miles. And yet, all I wanted on that day in May 1978, when I put on my shoes and stumbled through three miles, was to win back my girl.

Chapter 8

Connecting on the Trail

It was bright and cloudless, 9:00 a.m. and 24 degrees, when I parked at the Chamisa Trail trailhead on Hyde Park Road. We were in Santa Fe for the week while Cyndi attended a workshop, and I had planned a two-hour hike, my first long trail adventure in many months. I wanted to judge whether my five-month-old aftermarket knees were ready for my Iron Men church group's Guadalupe Peak hike in two weeks.

As I gathered my gear and studied the map, I noticed there were two mostly parallel trails. A large sign read "Alternate Route More Difficult." I decided the alternate route was the one for me; after all, this was intended to be a test.

While the regular trail followed the fall line across the face of the mountain, the Alternate Route climbed straight up the drainage, meaning there were several steep climbs. I was careful to keep from slipping and banging my new knees. The trail was still covered with snow from yesterday's storm, but I was using trekking poles to keep me stable on the ice.

For the first thirty minutes my hands were uncomfortably cold, painfully cold, even with my gloves. Still, it was a beautiful morning and an incredible hike. After about forty-five minutes I reached a trail junction where the alternate route joined the original Chamisa Trail as well as the Saddleback Trail, which, despite its name, followed a ridge line.

I followed the Saddleback Trail to the southwest for another fifteen minutes, sticking to my original plan to go out for an hour, then return. I wanted to give my knees a good test, but I also wanted to be able to function the rest of the day. Two hours seemed realistic.

After the turnaround, on the way back toward the trailhead, I kept thinking about that trail sign. Following our calling is never the easier trail. How often do I willingly take the "Alternate Route More Difficult" in my everyday life, not to make my journey harder but to make it significant? I've never been satisfied with a simple, easy hike through life but prefer to take on challenging projects day after day. The alternate route, the more difficult route, the meaningful route, calls out to me.

I spent years watching my parents live lives that were fully engaged with other people, giving away their talents and energy, choosing the Alternate Route More Difficult. And now, following family tradition, I myself feel called to help people live deeper lives with God. Even as I long for a simpler life, I know I'll never be happy if I'm not engaged with the Alternate Route.

♦ ♦ ♦ ♦ ♦

It's the backpacker's dilemma: we pack our fears. We load too much heavy gear into our packs, so we'll be prepared. Just in case.

The more discomfort we're afraid of, the more gear we pack, and the heavier our pack becomes. If we're afraid of the dark mountain night, we pack extra flashlights and batteries. If we're afraid of eating cold food, we pack extra fuel canisters. If we're afraid of getting rained on, we pack an extra change of clothes. If we're afraid of getting hungry, we pack extra food.

But a heavy pack is a danger of its own. It's exhausting to carry and alters our behavior on the trail by slowing us down, hindering good decisions, and draining our energy.

The good news is, with more experience we can overcome many of our fears. I've learned how much food I'll need on a three-day hike, so I don't carry too much. I've learned how many meals to expect from a fuel canister, so I don't weigh myself down with extras.

Other fears we learn to live with. I can suffer through a day in wet clothes, so I'll leave the extras behind. I can survive a night without a flashlight, so I'll leave the extra one at home. I can tolerate heavy hiking boots in the evening around camp, so I won't pack my cushy camp shoes.

It's a learning process, this constant winnowing of fears and gear. It takes a lifetime to get our pack weight down.

When I first began backpacking, I was convinced I had already packed as lightly as possible. Everything in my pack seemed necessary and useful. It took time on the trail to learn what I needed and what I didn't need. It took miles on the trail to know the difference between what was important for civilized survival and what was merely compensating for fear.

One Sunday morning in our adult Bible study class, we discussed a story found in Matthew 19 about Jesus and a rich young ruler. The story begins with the ruler asking a sincere and heartfelt question of Jesus: "What must I do to inherit eternal life?" The man wanted to do the right thing, and he asked the right person.

I picture the man holding his open checkbook and pen, the check already signed, ready to fill in the amount. He was willing to support Jesus's ministry, or sponsor a wing on the children's hospital, or give to the temple fund, or whatever Jesus asked.

However, after quizzing the man about his obedient lifestyle, Jesus surprised him with this request: "Sell everything you have and give it to the poor. Then follow me."

This was the last advice the man wanted to hear. It spoke to his deepest fears. How could he possibly give it all to the poor? Who would he be if he gave it all away? Who would listen to him if he weren't rich? How could he do great and mighty acts for the kingdom if he himself was poor? Where would the weight and significance of his life come from?

Hearing Jesus's expectations made the ruler sad. He had started the conversation with big hopes of doing something grand, but now all he could do was walk away.

The young ruler's backpack was full of fears: the fear that in the end he would be worse off than in the beginning; the fear he would lose more than he gained; the fear of financial insecurity; the fear of a life with no guarantees.

The man wanted to follow Jesus, but his backpack of fears was too heavy for the trail Jesus called him to hike.

When fear drives our behavior, we are not trusting God for our well-being. We must open our backpacks to God and release our grip on our own perfect gear for our own perfect hike.

♦ ♦ ♦ ♦ ♦

It was October 2003, and Cyndi and I were on our first hike up Guadalupe Peak, the highest elevation point in Texas. We were at the top enjoying lunch and looking through the logbook conveniently provided by the National Park Service, reading comments from other proud hikers. I asked Cyndi what she would write. Her eyes twinkled, and she said, "I wonder what sort of story we've stumbled into?" We had no idea we'd still be hiking this mountain seventeen years later. It turned out to be a big story after all.

Since that first hike with Cyndi, I've summited the Peak more than twenty times, yet the trail remains as hard as ever. It never gets easier. I keep asking myself the same question: Why am I still doing this?

Climbing to the top of a mountain is a satisfying experience. There is a definite goal to achieve, and the goal is easy to evaluate. You know for certain when you're at the top. But hiking to the top of this mountain is not easy. The first hour is hot and steep and hard, a series of rocky switchbacks that gain elevation step after step. It is enough to send most casual hikers back down to their car. All you can do is put your head down and keep moving. There is no quick way to the top, no shortcuts, no secret passageways for people who buy the expensive tickets. You can't conquer the Peak by reading or studying or going to workshops; you must hike with your own two feet, and it is hard work.

I enjoy taking groups up Guadalupe Peak; it's a metaphor for how we achieve the most valuable things in life. The trail is hard and long with no shortcuts or quick fixes. Kathleen Norris described my own thoughts in her book *Dakota: A Spiritual Geography*: "Enlightenment can't be found in a weekend workshop. There is no such a thing as becoming an instantly spiritualized person." She continued, "Americans seek the quick fix for spiritual as well as physical growth. The fact that conversion is a lifelong process is the last thing we want to hear."[15]

I'm also attracted to the Guadalupe Mountains because of the view. It's spectacular—breathtaking in its raw unconcern for the hiker. As you stand at the summit and gaze across the Chihuahuan Desert for a hundred miles, you see nothing friendly to man, nothing that cares whether humans cross. The desert is complete, self-contained, and stingy, offering no comforts to soothe a human being. Oddly enough, that indifference speaks to my heart. From Barbara Kingsolver: "Looking out on a clean plank of planet earth, we can get shaken right down to the bone by the bronze-eyed possibility of lives that are not our own."[16] I need to be regularly reminded that I'm not the center of life, and this desert convinces me better than anything else.

Hiking these mountains reminds my fellow hikers and me that we can push through almost anything hard, difficult, or painful if we have a compelling reason to not give up. During the last 25 percent of the hike, when we're all exhausted, our feet are sore, we're dehydrated and long out of water, and we can see the parking lot way down there, but there is no shortcut back to the bus and no faster way down the mountain—even then, we keep moving.

Later, once we are all off the mountain, settled into our seats for the long drive back to Midland, the bus buzzing with stories, injuries, photos, and hearts joining together—that part of the trip is one of my favorite times of the day. Sharing our stories makes us brothers.

I often say, "Without a scar, we don't have a story." It's in the disasters, the injuries, the surviving, that our character is revealed, and what starts as a set of mere incidents morphs from timeline into story.

Since that October day with Cyndi in 2003, the trail up Guadalupe Peak has become one of my most important paths. From it I've learned God speaks to me most often when I'm moving and when I'm vulnerable. Dirt trails have become a big part of my spiritual journey and being on top of mountains helps keep my eyes open to the larger, wider, wilder world.

♦ ♦ ♦ ♦ ♦

Early Monday morning, Labor Day 2018, Cyndi, our friend Clark, and I left Williams Lake (elevation 11,040 feet) and hiked down to my pickup at the trailhead, put on clean, dry clothes, and made the five-hundred-mile drive home through Taos, Santa Fe, Roswell, Plains, Seminole, and Midland.

We'd spent the previous two nights at Williams Lake, and it rained all night the second night. It was cold but never got down to freezing. I was proud of Cyndi—she was uncomfortably cold the entire time the whole trip, from parking lot to parking lot. For Clark and I, the climb up to Wheeler Peak at altitude was the hardest part of the trip. For Cyndi, that was the easy part; the cold was hardest on her.

At 13,161 feet above sea level, Wheeler Peak is the highest mountain in New Mexico. Located in the Sangre De Cristo range at the southern end of the Rocky Mountains, it invites all to enjoy its majesty.

This was our first ascent of Wheeler Peak, and it was grand. The trail from Williams Lake to the summit is about five miles round trip and is ranked as a steep and difficult class 2 trail, with the final mile-and-a-half a series of switchbacks crisscrossing a rocky scree slope. The rocks never felt dangerous, even if the trail was often uncomfortable and slippery. It was well-maintained and not as dicey as I expected after reading online trail accounts.

We spent about thirty minutes at the summit, taking photos, eating lunch, signing the logbook, and laughing at the college guys who lost the trail and were forced to scramble straight up the scree slope.

We started down at the sound of approaching thunder, moving slowly at first. Descending is technically more difficult than ascending. During the climb up, your foot is planted before your body weight is shifted. The opposite is true on descent, and it's less stable. Descent is basically a controlled fall, which is why most mountaineering accidents happen during the descent. It pays to be careful.

We made it back to camp as the sky opened with rain and hail; we all got free afternoon naps in our tents while waiting out the storm. Later, after the rain stopped and we cooked our dinner, we talked about a term I read in Scott Jurek's book *North*. It was the idea of elective suffering,[17] that we put ourselves though hard activities simply because we want to. Cindy, Clark, and I are lucky to live lives that allow this. We have enough discretionary time and money. So why choose to use our freedom to hike and tent-camp in the cold and wet? I don't know, except to say there is value in elective suffering. There is the joy of success, a sense of accomplishment, and the camaraderie of shared experience.

But beyond that, there is added value in going beyond the casual effort. It amplifies the focus and risk and spiritual connection.

Backpacking connects me to God. Even more than hiking. I love the day hikes we do, but they connect me with people, especially other men. Backpacking is different because there is more risk involved, more uncertainty, more opportunities for things to go wrong, more ways to be miserable for a day or two. And that risk, along with the isolation of the outback, opens me up to God, focuses me in some way, quiets my mental chatter,

♦ ♦ ♦ ♦ ♦

One Saturday I was blessed to join my friend David hiking in McKittrick Canyon. The canyon trail is famous for two things: (1) it's the only easy hike in the Guadalupe Mountains National Park, and (2) it's surprisingly, brilliantly colorful in early November.

In general, nature couldn't care less if we enjoy the view, and it makes minimal effort to carve an easy path for us. But McKittrick Canyon is an exception, a gift from God.

The hike is about seven miles round trip and is easy enough for young families. There were plenty of youngsters on the trail and a few hikers older than either David or me, if you can believe that.

This was meant to be a larger hiking group. I had twenty on my list the preceding Monday and had reserved a sixteen-passenger church bus. But what I knew would happen, happened: family life took its toll, and one by one people dropped off the list, all with good reasons—weddings to attend, soccer games rescheduled, illness, tickets to a (losing) college football game. By Friday my list had dwindled to two hikers: David and me.

Life is all about choices, and we're continually choosing between good options. As adults, and as parents, we must consider the whole family when choosing how to spend our Saturdays, so I wasn't disappointed that people chose to do something else. But I had a choice to make too. Should we go with only two people or cancel the trip? The canyon is three and a half hours from Midland, a seven-hour round trip, and we all have plenty to do on a Saturday.

However, I didn't want to cancel. I'd already bailed on one hike two months earlier for the same reason, and I didn't want to do it again. I also knew David had been planning for this for a long time. Besides being a great friend and fellow Bible teacher, David is in long recovery from a near-fatal heart attack. Back in the old days, before his attack, he joined us on much more difficult hikes to the summit of Guadalupe Peak. I wanted to be part of his return to the trails.

The best time for hiking McKittrick Canyon is the last week of October and first week of November, when the changing leaves offer the most vivid and striking colors. In the middle of the arid desert mountains, the canyon surprises hikers with oak trees, ash trees, and bigtooth maples. It's a pretty place to be any time of the year, but in the fall, when bright yellow and dark maroon leaves stand out against the gray-brown landscape, it's stunning.

At one of the water crossings, we waited in line for the one set of steppingstones. A hiker was struggling to hold her balance as she tiptoed across the rocks, swaying from side to side like a beginning tightrope walker. She made it without falling. The curious thing was, she had a trekking pole in her hand, which she held aloft for balance. If she had planted the pole on the bottom of the stream with each step, used it as it was intended, her journey would have been much quicker, safer, and less frightening. I considered hollering to her about using her pole, but no one wants unsolicited advice while working their way across a stream.

How many of us struggle through life trying not to lose our balance and topple into the water, when we're holding in our hands the exact equipment we need to make the trip stable and safe?

The same situation appears in the movie *A Walk in the Woods*[18] when the two senior-in-age-but-not-in-experience hikers, Bryson and Katz, try to cross a wild river. Both end up losing their balance and falling into the water, backpacks and all. Every time I see that scene, it's all I can do to keep from yelling at the screen (Cyndi would say I occasionally do yell), "Use the trekking poles you have strapped to your backpacks, you fools! Why carry them all along the Appalachian Trail if you don't use them when crossing a river?"

We've been given everything we need to navigate the rocky streams of life. Second Peter 1:3 says, "His divine power has given us everything we need for a godly life through our knowledge of him who called us by his own glory and goodness."

God doesn't promise we won't slip into the water, or slide off one of the rocks, or sneeze and lose our balance as we are stretching for a long step to the bank. But he does promise us everything we need to live a godly life. It's up to us to use what he's given, live out his calling, rely on his mercy and grace, believe his promises, and stop leaving them in our backpacks for another day.

That Saturday in McKittrick Canyon, I enjoyed two of God's greatest gifts, both of which I need for a godly life. One was time on the trail surrounded by wild beauty, and the other was extended time with my friend David. I tell Cyndi often,

"Too many men go through life without one single quality friend, and I have dozens—more than my share." The hike in the canyon was fun, but more than that, it was an honor to share the trail with one of my guys.

Chapter 9

What I Learn from Cycling

One breezy February morning in 2018 I rode in a cycling club 100K fun ride, the furthest I'd even thought about riding for two years. Following my double knee replacement about eight months prior, I'd been making incremental increases up the distance ladder. That approach made good sense physically and helped me avoid injury, but it did little to energize my thinking. I expected this ride to open my mind as well as give my knees a substantial test.

Unfortunately, I made the rookie mistake of starting out too fast and trying to hang with the lead group longer than I should have. But I did that on purpose since most of my rides are alone; I seldom get a sense of how much more energy I should invest when I'm riding by myself. I knew I couldn't stay with the lead pace all day, but I pushed hard to stay with them if I could.

The good news from the ride was my knees felt great. They weren't the limiting factor for the day. What slowed me down were my lungs. I couldn't ride the pace with the rest of the group and still breathe.

In truth, with full disclosure, I didn't complete the entire 100K. I was tired and defeated at the two-hour mark, which was also when the ride director suggested everyone turn around and head back home, so I uncharacteristically followed instructions and turned around.

Riding back toward Midland was much harder than riding away. I fought against the strong southeast wind blowing against my right shoulder for miles, getting slower and slower, until another rider rode up beside me. Jeff is about eight feet tall and creates a formidable wind break. He maneuvered to the right-hand side of the road, between me and the wind, and motioned for me to tuck into his draft. He pulled me for the next ten miles and would not let me fall off the pace. In fact, whenever I started to fade, he slowed down to catch me and bring me back to speed

By the time I finished the day I had fifty-eight miles, four miles shy of a 100K. I wasn't disappointed; this was a significant jump in distance for me, and I was happy to finish on my own two wheels. I accomplished all my objectives of the day: my knees felt great, and while my legs were shot, I could still stand up and walk around.

As I loaded my bike into the pickup bed, I heard the other guys talk about their Sunday morning plan. The next morning they were riding to Kermit and back, about 140 miles round trip. It was a bit overwhelming to hear, knowing I was done for the weekend, but it gave me a better picture of what's possible. I couldn't do what they planned to do at the time, but someday.

There is a hardness that comes only from extended time in the saddle. I don't mean butt or quad hardness but mental hardness. And it doesn't come any other way except from riding long distances on a regular basis and letting other riders pull you up to speed.

It's also true for running, backpacking, and even yoga. My wife Cyndi can do back-to-back, day-long workshops, at a master level, when I can barely last through a one-hour class. She's put in the extended time on her mat. She's toughened up. And she's let other people pull her up.

While my regular twenty-mile rides meet the need for cardiovascular exercise and weight management, they do little to inspire me. I learned in my old pre-knee-surgery life that it was the long training runs of two hours or more that reshaped my thoughts and opened my mind. I had to run far enough to find the meditation point. Now that I'm cycling, I must ride far enough.

The Bible says, "When troubles of any kind come your way, consider it an opportunity for great joy. For you know that when your faith is tested, your endurance has a chance to grow" (James 1:2–3 NLT). We cannot grow without trouble, and we will not grow without perseverance. The good news is, we don't have to endure on our own. We don't have to fight the headwinds by ourselves. We can draft behind those who are stronger and let them pull us. We can borrow faith from each other when life gets hard. Pull up close and let your brother or sister block the wind.

♦ ♦ ♦ ♦ ♦

The northwest wind was significant, and I knew I'd have to fight it the entire way, but I'd been dormant long enough. I needed to move.

I was riding my regular route to Greentree only to discover the main boulevard was being rebuilt. Half the road in both directions had been scraped down to the caliche base, meaning I'd have to bump across a three-inch deep canyon and dodge giant road-building equipment. I was certainly on the wrong bike for that sort of thing, so I modified my route using the unaltered roads and found the distance I was looking for.

Pleased with my problem-solving ability and manly wind-fighter legs, I headed back home on Wood Street. About two blocks east of Midland Drive, I looked to the northern horizon and saw an epic Dust Bowl Days wall of sand blowing toward Midland. It was frightening, so the first thing I did was stop and take a photo, since no difficult task or situation goes undocumented nowadays. Then I stood up on my pedals and took off for home. Could I make it home before the sand overtook me? We'd soon find out.

A couple of drivers slowed as they passed me, lowering their windows and shouting advice while pointing at the approaching storm, assuming, I suppose, I hadn't noticed it or else I wouldn't be out riding. They wanted to talk to me, but I had no time for conversation. I was in a race against nature.

I almost made it. I was about a half-mile from my house when the headwind and sand hit me full on, instantly dropping my speed from fifteen miles an hour to seven.

Here's the thing: It makes no sense to complain about the wind or sand. Having lived in West Texas for fifty-five of my sixty-three years, I have no excuses. Only a fool would be surprised about something as permanent and persistent as the wind. I either keep my bike in the garage until perfectly calm days, which are few, or take on the challenge.

Through the years I've learned most of my creativity comes from turbulence. I doubt I'd have much to write about if life suddenly went laminar. After an essay or two about how peaceful I felt, I would be done.

My pursuit of God is born in turbulence too. I'm afraid I would forget about God if I didn't have to beg him for help regularly, every time I felt the wind and sand in my face.

♦ ♦ ♦ ♦ ♦

Last week's bike ride near Durango, Colorado, wouldn't have lit me up the same way had it been thirty miles on straight, flat roads like the ones I ride all the time at home in Texas. It was the twenty-mile descent and eight-mile climb that gave me a story and made the ride worth hauling my bike all the way up from Midland to Colorado in the back of Cyndi's car.

I rode the same route twice, Sunday and Tuesday, and on both occasions, I had to stop partway up the climb. My legs were tired, and my lungs were drained. I unclipped from the pedals, laid my chest on the handlebars, and tried to breathe and not throw up. The first day, I was audibly gasping when a young rider dressed in black rode right past me, dancing in his pedals directly up the same road that had broken me. In my defense, I was thirty years older and thirty pounds heavier, and I wasn't use to biking at that height. I live at 2,782 feet elevation, where the air is abundant, instead of 8,222 feet, where it isn't.

I wasn't embarrassed about being passed as much as I was jealous. The truth is, no matter what you do, there is someone who does it better and easier. Cyndi was once passed during the Boston Marathon by a guy running backwards and then by another guy wearing an Old North Church costume. I was passed in the New York City Marathon by a guy juggling three tennis balls. There is always someone.

My Durango adventure wasn't an epic bike ride in the world of cycling, but for me, in my current state of fitness, in my current state of age, in my current state of training, it was huge. If I lived in Colorado and rode every day, I would be making hard climbs regularly. But I don't, and I don't, so I can't.

I didn't do hard rides exclusively. While in Durango I spent more time writing and reading while seated comfortably alongside the Animas River than I did riding my bike. But trying something hard is important to me. And having a story to tell is even more important. My writing is better, closer to the bone, if I invest first in cycling or running or hiking. It grounds me, settles my thoughts.

♦ ♦ ♦ ♦ ♦

I rode with Brian yesterday at 5:00 p.m. It was 103 degrees when we left my house for a twenty-mile ride.

Brian was among the tribe of voices, along with my brother Carroll and friends Mark, David H., David N., and Todd, who convinced me to try cycling when arthritis had damaged my knees too much for running. I quickly learned I could push myself on my bike and work my heart and lungs the way I used to when running. My knees didn't hurt while I was on my bike, or later after I got off it. I also learned, or remembered, how much fun it was to ride long and fly through the air.

When I first started riding, in June 2010, Brian was racing a lot. He was my hammerhead example and a rider I admired and looked up to. I didn't plan on racing—I felt too late to the game for that—but he had a big influence on me. I remember he loaned me his collection of bike saddles so I could try them one by one to see which style worked best for me.

So when he sent a message asking if I wanted to ride, I was both happy and nervous. I knew it would be hot, but Brian lives in Saudi Arabia now and is used to hotter conditions than I am—and I regularly ride at above 100 degrees in the Texas summer. The question was, could I keep up? But since he broached the subject, I figured he was already prepared to ride at my pace.

It was a fun ride and we did lots of visiting and catching up—that is, when the wind wasn't blowing in our ears and cars weren't zooming loudly past.

I'm stronger when I'm with someone else.

♦ ♦ ♦ ♦ ♦

A few minutes ago, I got off my bike from a warm and windy April ride and started working on these stories. Like everyone else in the world, I've been stuck working from home and severely limiting my outside trips due to the COVID-19 epidemic. My best survival tool so far has been a daily run or ride. No one gets closer than thirty feet during either adventure, so I feel I'm keeping enough social distance.

I've learned from past crises that I stay on point best when I commit to daily disciplines. The practices I try to do every day—read from my Daily Bible, write in my journal, ride, or run—take on even more importance when the rest of life gets wobbly.

It's hard being by myself all day, even for an introverted loner like me. I'm stronger when I'm with someone else.

Part Three

SHARING
What I Learn

Chapter 10

Telling Stories of Life

I've wondered if I would enjoy the monastic life. Being alone and spending my days reading and studying, writing and praying, sounds pretty good to me. The idea of unlimited time to develop my thoughts and work through ideas is very attractive.

But real monks don't seem to spend that much time reading, writing, and studying. If that was all they do, they would starve to death within a few weeks. Monks spend most of their time working, just like everyone else. Everyone has to earn a living. Most accounts of monastic life tell of hard labor and hot work in the fields or the kitchen all day, every day . . . and of rising at 4:00 a.m. for morning prayer . . . and of meeting for worship five or six times daily. Monks may be isolated from the outside world, but they hardly live in solitude. A monastery is a tight community of people living their whole lives close to each other.

That isn't what I wanted. A monk's life didn't seem to leave much room for expression or individuality, and I would have a problem with that. And besides, wives aren't allowed in monasteries, and I would be miserable without Cyndi. The whole celibate thing trumped all the benefits, if you ask me.

But the idea of holing up by myself had always sounded good.

One Thursday morning I found myself sitting on a big rock perched on the lip of a box canyon in the badlands southwest of Iraan, Texas. I was under a tree, in the shade, watching for rattlesnakes and waiting for a wireline truck to finish running the perforating guns into the casing of a gas well I was working on. A cool breeze was blowing, and I was writing in my journal. It was so quiet and peaceful and stimulating to be sitting there by myself, I wondered if I could be happy living as a hermit in the back of one of these canyons. That is, if I had an ample supply of food, water, shade, books, and of course, running shoes.

Louis L'Amour wrote, in his autobiography Education of a Wandering Man, about a time when he was hired to guard a mine that lay in a basin at the end of thirty-odd miles of winding, one-lane dirt road in remote southern California. There was a concrete bunkhouse to live in. L'Amour's boss dropped him off in front of the bunkhouse and drove away, leaving Louis all by himself. He wrote, "It was not Walden Pond. There was no water here except what came from a well. There were no forests. There wasn't a tree within miles."[19] But there were boxes of books left by the previous occupant, and Louis L'Amour devoured them. He said the loneliness never affected him because he was so busy reading.

Well, that sounded a lot better than being a monk: minimal obligations, plenty to eat and drink, unlimited time to read, and time to go for a long run every day. I wouldn't even have to fight for survival, like Tom Hanks in the movie Cast Away, and

I wouldn't have been without books or paper. I could really be alone, thinking and reading.

But as I sat on that rock and contemplated the uninhabited canyon in front of me, I knew I wouldn't be happy living that way for long. Besides the fact that I couldn't be happy without Cyndi, I realized I was never totally happy learning and studying and analyzing unless I had an opportunity to share what I'd learned. It wasn't enough to do something; I wanted to tell my stories afterward. Somehow the sharing was part of the learning process, as if I wouldn't have room to learn more unless I passed along what I already knew.

So, while I dreamed of a hermit's life of solitude, I knew it was a mythical, idealistic image I'd created. Sure, I could live alone—but I didn't want to live alone. I couldn't imagine a life without Cyndi, and I couldn't imagine learning anything new and different and not having someone to share it with. What a waste that would be. It was in the sharing that I really learned what I knew, and it was the opportunity to share that made me want to learn more. That was the source of my joy in teaching—the chance to give away what I'd learned. It couldn't be done living alone in the desert.

♦ ♦ ♦ ♦ ♦

One of my favorite writers and teachers of writing, Natalie Goldberg, is a devout Buddhist. She wrote often about her Zen teacher—the lessons he taught and the way he lived. The two were seamless; there was complete unity in his talk and his walk.

Natalie said when she first started listening to her teacher, she had no idea what he was talking about. She couldn't tell friends what she'd heard because she was so lost at understanding it. But she kept coming back because she felt, she knew, there was value and depth and light there, and she needed more of that. She saw it in his life.

I want to be a teacher like that: the information I share and the life I live working hand-in-hand, each reinforcing the other, each giving value and truth to the other.

♦ ♦ ♦ ♦ ♦

I was sitting in our kitchen reading *Tracks of a Fellow Struggler* by John R. Claypool while Cyndi baked and decorated cookies. I read this paragraph to Cyndi: "I had come to the conclusions, that it was the nature of God to speak to us in the *language of events*, and that it was the nature of the church for human beings to share with each other what they thought they had heard God say in the things that had happened to them."[20]

She knew why I read it immediately. I said, "This describes not only everything I write, every story I tell, as well as my motivation behind it, but tells it better than I could ever say it. I believe it is my calling, my charge, to tell stories in the language of events, putting truth within reach."

She nodded and smiled in approval. She agreed exactly.

I once remarked that my writing covers so many areas, I'm unsure whether any consistent message comes across. Am I wasting my time? Should I be more deliberate?

She disagreed. She said the *Love Song* CDs I made as giveaways to friends over the years tell people about our love for each other and God's love for us, regardless of whether I explicitly mention it. And posting in my Facebook cartoon collection[21] tells the story of observation and clever fun and joy of life, and it tells of God. Writing stories and insights from running or cycling demonstrates how God speaks to us in the things that happen to us. She is a smart woman.

Cyndi rattled off names of four or five teachers at our church and said they teach the way they do because they've been around me. She told me that teachers all over our church have been influenced by the way I use personal stories, movie clips, and popular references so effectively.

It was a big deal hearing Cyndi say that, and I haven't stopped thinking about it. I am grateful for any influence God has given me.

We need to hear things like that from other people, especially people we love and respect. For we are not good judges of our own influence, and we seldom know and understand what we do best.

♦ ♦ ♦ ♦ ♦

After running along part of the Trinity River Trail in Fort Worth, I recovered by reading from my Daily Bible, Exodus 3–4, about Moses's call to action—to leadership, to ministry—at the burning bush in the desert.

A reluctant Moses asked, "What if they don't believe or listen to me?"

God replied, "What's that in your hand."

I expect Moses checked both hands closely before answering, wondering what God was up to. Did God see something in his hand he didn't know about? Was this a trick question? Moses was holding his shepherd's staff, but he was always holding that. It was so familiar. It was part of his arm. Why would God ask what was in his hand when it was something that was always in his hand?

I imagine Moses raising his eyebrows and his voice in a question when he said, "A staff?" He didn't even call it "my staff." Why would God be interested in the most ordinary thing he had?

We all have things in our hand that define us, that are our strength, but are so familiar to us that we tend to forget about them.

"What's that in your hand, Berry?"

"My pen."

"My journal."

"My teaching notes."

"My trekking poles."

"My trombone."

"My list of jokes."

"My very cool spreadsheets"

"My daily checklists"

It's all regular, daily stuff. No big deal.

Oh?

In a devastatingly personal encounter during a 2008 men's retreat, God confronted me in no uncertain terms with the message: "You don't know how big it is."

Curiously, and much to my dismay, God gave no details about what he meant by "it." I had to figure that out on my own, but it seemed obvious "it" was something I was underestimating. Something that was part of my everyday life—the staff in my hand, so to speak.

After God called attention to Moses's staff, a simple shepherd's tool, he told Moses to throw it on the ground.

Throw it down? The thing Moses leaned on, depended on for support and protection while tending sheep in the Midian wilderness? The thing that was so much a part of him that he never gave it a second thought—throw it down?

Yes, Moses. Throw it down. Never mind why; just give it up. Trust God enough to surrender the thing you're hanging on to.

Moses obeyed, and what followed was a striking display of what can happen when a person submits the ordinary stuff of life to God. Moses certainly was convinced—enough that, complying with God's direction, he took his wife and sons and started back to Egypt.

With him went "the staff of God" (Exodus 4:20). No one thought it an ordinary shepherd's tool now. God had called attention to it, then taken it away. And when he gave it back to Moses, it had new significance. Now it was God's staff; Moses just got to carry it for him.

Oh, and use it to produce water from a rock. And watch it transform into a snake in front of Pharaoh. And hold it aloft to win the battle of Rephidim.

As with all Bible stories, we have to ask, is this one only about Moses? Could it be about us as well? Would God point out something he has given to us—a gift, a blessing, a talent, a skill, a calling, a ministry—and then tell us to throw it down?

Would God ask us to throw down something that has defined us, established our identity and worth, with no indication of what would happen next? Would God say to me, "You don't know how big this is. Now throw it down"?

♦ ♦ ♦ ♦ ♦

I recently gave my church's education minister and my class director my one-year notice that I intended to stop teaching on a regular basis. The next September would mark my thirtieth year of teaching adult Bible study, and it seemed the appropriate time. I told them I love teaching and would be happy to continue as a substitute when a class needed one. I'd also be glad to team teach to give a new teacher experience and familiarity with the class members. But I was ready to step back from my weekly assignment, and I was also willing to leave sooner if they found someone ready to take over.

The decision is one I had been thinking about for several months. Once I made it, I gave myself the entire summer to dwell on it, pray about it, and give God plenty of opportunity to change my mind.

For an hour or two following my conversation with the ministry heads, I felt flat, mentally and emotionally washed out, as if I'd cycled a hundred miles. I had no remorse or second guessing, nor yet a sense of relief, as if I'd finally gotten it over with. I was simply blank, as if my bodily systems had shut down to let me catch my breath.

Teaching has been my identity since 1990. I have taught Bible class longer than I was in government, longer than I've written journals, and twice the length of my lengthiest job. Thirty years is more than half my adult life, and it doesn't count my years teaching while in college and when Cyndi and I first married. Altogether, I've been a teacher longer than I've been a runner, a husband, a father, and an engineer.

My decision didn't feel like I abandoned a responsibility, or dodged a bullet, or left something undone. I had no disagreements or bones to pick with anyone. It felt more like I was getting out of the way, clearing the deck for the next generation to step forward.

It also felt like I'd turned the corner, as if an internal, emotional GPS were telling me my next exit was in one year. The next phase of life was approaching. And I was asking God to change my heart and prepare me for whatever he had next.

It felt like moving on.

Chapter 11

Experiencing the Sacred

I spent Saturday afternoon strolling around downtown Santa Fe looking for any of several bookstores that popped up when I pressed my Around Me app. But no joy—either the data was stale or the bookstores were too well hidden. Hiding a bookstore makes no sense if the owner intends to sell books, unless it's a Harry Potter bookstore. Or unless it's in Santa Fe, where businesses relish being hard to find and impossible to park near.

Hoping to redeem my time spent not locating a bookstore, I walked inside St. Francis Basilica to sit in a pew for a short while. The cathedral has a nice bookstore, so I suppose I found what I was looking for, but I had already been there many times before and bought all the books I was interested in.

After a few minutes of sitting and writing, I lifted my head out of my Moleskine journal and noticed a couple dozen tourists inside. I was the only one not taking a selfie. Of course, I felt noble and righteous about that; my own phone was reverently stowed in my back pocket. However, as I sat in judgment of the selfie takers, it occurred to me how un-Saint-Francis-like it was to feel nobler than them.

Taking a selfie is not unholy or irreverent. We all experience the sacred in our own way. Who knows the stories of all these people? Maybe some of them recently turned their lives around, and entered a church for the first time ever, and documented the experience for themselves and their support group. Or maybe one of them had promised a photo for a dying aunt who wanted to attend this church her entire. I'm sure many of those selfie takers wondered why a gray-haired man would sit alone in a cathedral writing in his journal. Was their method of documenting the experience less righteous than mine, they might ask?

♦ ♦ ♦ ♦ ♦

I read from Isaiah 30, including verse 21: "Your ears will hear a voice behind you, saying, 'This is the way, walk in it.'"

In the margin of my Bible, I've written a list of messages I heard from God over the years, as plain and clear as if there were a person behind me speaking into my ears. They aren't the only ones; they're just maybe the ones with enough seasons behind them to give me the courage to write them down in my Bible.

"Marry Cyndi." "You should be teaching." "You have something to say." "Stay where you are." "Dude, go for a run." "Sell some stuff." These tiny whispers seem unimportant, even cryptic, when I list them out like this, but each one spoke directly into my life when I heard it.

Once in June 2013, I sat in a rocking chair on my friend Sam Williamson's front porch in Anne Arbor, Michigan, and asked

God to reveal to me the purpose and meaning he had embedded in me. As I prayed, I said aloud, "I don't want to find God, standing alone." It wouldn't be enough to learn my life calling, or sell thousands of books, or teach so many classes, unless I could see a wake of changed lives traveling alongside. I wrote the phrase in my Bible so I would be reminded every year when I read that passage.

♦ ♦ ♦ ♦ ♦

We talk too much about clarity, how we are seeking it in a situation or in a decision. Not only is clarity rare and elusive, it's also subjective and highly overrated. Instead of solving problems, it leaves us wanting still more clarity beyond whatever we may get.

I can't think of any decision Cyndi I ever made when we were clear about what we should do, clear about God's direction, clear about what to expect.

Maybe one of the clearest decisions I can think of was running for reelection in 2007. After serving for twelve years as the District Four representative on the city council, I felt certain God was calling me, expecting me, to run for the at-large seat. To me it was as clear as any decision I'd been faced with up to that point in my life. I had complete peace in choosing to run.

But I lost the election, resulting in a minor crisis of faith for me. Well, not exactly a crisis. I never doubted God's call for me to run. I knew he didn't promise I would win. But I didn't understand why he called me to campaign so I would lose in front of the whole town.

In my career as an engineer, working for many local companies, none of those job changes felt like clarity. I would say my decision to work for Amerada Hess in 1979, when Cyndi and I were starting out, was the only job I ever accepted where I was thinking of a long-term career. All the others—a collection of major and independent oil companies in Midland—felt like temporary solutions to me when I started, like placeholder jobs I could take advantage of until God's real plan was ready. I didn't see clearly how God used them in my life until years afterward.

Even in retrospect I seldom see much clarity. I can analyze old decisions and see how eventually they worked out to advantage, but that is more about redeeming the past than clearly understanding my story.

I remember when we borrowed money to build Cyndi's new yoga studio. It was a little unnerving, even though both of us felt it was the right and best thing to do. Cyndi said, "Well, if it all falls apart and we lose money, we'll figure it out and move on. At least we'll still have each other. We won't be by ourselves"—a key, if rare, grown-up attitude.

I believe Cyndi and I have become more comfortable with uncertainty as we get older—probably because we trust each other more but even more because we trust God's character. And because we trust God, we trust our own intuition about decisions. We're more comfortable saying, "Let's do this and see what happens" because God has been faithful for so long.

♦ ♦ ♦ ♦

Do you have gifts and talents you underestimate? The correct answer is: Yes, you do. We all do.

We typically don't recognize or understand our most powerful talents on our own. We need to hear from friends and family. In fact, it's unlikely we'll ever understand our calling or purpose without counsel from people who are close around us.

But we get glimpses, and for me they often come through music or movies.

Cyndi and I usually watch a movie in the evening while working on stuff like family finances, writing the next book, managing a mobile home park, or running a yoga studio. We tend to pick movies we've seen many times so we can follow along without being distracted by a story we don't already know. And much to nephew Kevin's dismay, when he is with us, as he often is, we typically choose nonexploding, nonfighting movies.

So, we watched August Rush again. I've seen this movie many times since my first viewing at a Wild at Heart Advanced Camp in May 2008, where it changed almost everything about my life, so I didn't expect it to affect me the same way as it has in the past. I supposed I'd built up some immunity.

I was wrong. The movie nailed me once again, and I had to go sit by myself in my closet (I have a rocking chair in there) and absorb the message. Specifically, I internalized what God was saying to me before I let it get away.

A lot of movies dig emotional responses out of me. No, that's too weak a statement. A lot of movies make me cry. And each year the list of movies gets longer, either because I'm better at picking out movies or because I'm getting softer. August Rush is one of those; it slips past the bare patch of my armored chest like Bard's black arrow in The Hobbit and sticks directly into my heart.

The movie is about a young, orphaned boy named August Rush, a musical prodigy, who uses music to reach out to the parents he hopes to find. Only, when I watch it, it isn't about music but about writing and teaching.

In the movie, when a man asks August, "What do you want to be?" he answers with one word: "Found." Not being lost is profound, and watching this movie helps me realize it's my job to find people and lead them on the trail so they won't be lost.

But the scene that penetrates my armor is when the head of a music conservatory asks young August, "Where does the music come from?" He answers, "It's like someone is calling out to me. Writing it all down is like I'm calling back to them."[22] This is exactly what writing feels like to me.

After the movie finished I sat in my rocking chair in my closet with tears rolling down my cheeks, praying, "I'm sorry. I don't know how big it is.

"I'm sorry I continually underestimate what you've given to me. Because I don't speak to big crowds or sell tons of books or have thousands of readers, I underestimate the gift and the result. Thank you for giving me so many turns. Thank you for lighting the fire inside to teach and write and give away and improve. Thank you for sharing insights and connections. I want to give them back to you."

Here's the thing. None of us understands our own influence. None of us knows how big it is because we don't pay attention the same way God does. We don't notice the same results God sees. We don't see hearts the same way God does—we are stuck in this present day, but God sees the long-term benefit. All we can know is, we aren't the heroes of our own stories, no matter how big. The heroes are the people who respond, who stand up and step forward, and we are simply lucky to be part of the story.

Chapter 12

Grace Abounds

For the past few years Cyndi and I have traveled with the Metro Big Band, Cyndi on percussion and congas, me on trombone. The Metro Big Band is an eighteen-piece jazz ensemble based in the United States, led by Camp Kirkland, that travels to various locations around the world. Finding this ministry was a delight after all our years in music. It has reenergized our love of music and deepened our understanding of the many ways we can share the love of Jesus.

On our trip to Guatemala, we worked with Coro Philharmonic, an organization in Guatemala City that rescues kids and young adults from street gangs and violent homes by teaching them to be musicians. The director explained: in this avalanche of sin, grace abounds through music.

One Sunday afternoon we drove to the church in Villa Nueva, Guatemala—the Green Church, as we called it, because it was painted bright neon green. The members were in their seats, patiently waiting for us as we set up on the small, crowded stage. Knowing how loud we were, I was concerned that the first row of people were only about six feet in the front of the band.

For our church concerts we included several hymns in our set so the congregation could sing along with us. We played "How Great Is Our God/How Great Thou Art" and "Great Is Thy Faithfulness." The people loved it, singing with heads back and mouths wide open. It was a joy to be with these passionate souls and their robust singing.

During "Great Is Thy Faithfulness," I noticed a woman about two rows back, probably in her seventies, with long silver hair pulled into a loose ponytail, eyes closed and arms in the air, singing with full emotion and energy and weeping huge tears. Here was a woman who understood the faithfulness of God. Of course, as soon as I saw her, I started crying too, which made it hard to keep playing since I couldn't see my music. The scene reminded me of author Kathleen Norris's observation about old women and their well-worn Bibles: there is more to this than you know.

♦ ♦ ♦ ♦ ♦

The musicians in the Metro Big Band come from all over the country. They tend to be middle-aged or retired adults who can afford the time away from home and who have lived many years playing music.

The charts are emailed to us about four weeks before the tour, which means we're expected to learn them before we leave home. The first time the band rehearses together is our first evening in our destination country. Our first concert is the next day.

When Cyndi and I traveled with the orchestral version of this ministry, I made it through the first night of rehearsals feeling good about it all. We were exhausted from the flight to Israel and two long hours of rehearsing, but we both felt up to the challenge of the music.

However, that first night in Guatemala with the jazz band was different. From the very beginning, the very first song, I felt like a little boy in a roomful of adults. I was intimidated by the musicianship and the rapid learning curve. The first couple of songs we pulled out scared me, not because the music was too fast or too impossible (which it was on both counts) but because everyone in the band was so much better than I was—better than I'll ever be. Better than I could've ever been had I dedicated my life to it.

After rehearsal, I texted about my fears and insecurity to my friend Rabon Bewley, saxophonist and music professor at Midland College, who has traveled with this group on at least a dozen international trips. He gently talked me off the ledge and promised it would get better, less frightening, as the tour proceeded. And after I got a night or two of sleep.

As the week progressed, with a half-dozen successful concerts behind me, I began to feel better about my playing. I was beginning to settle in. My confidence grew with each performance, and by the end of the week I felt, well, still out of my league, but comfortable playing with the band. I knew I was contributing in a positive way. And I was having fun.

Even with all my personal angst, I loved watching Cyndi play congas and growing into her own confidence. It was probably the first time in our years together that both of us had to struggle with inadequacy and fear at the same time, together.

Was it a bonding experience? Maybe, but I don't recommend it for anyone.

♦ ♦ ♦ ♦ ♦

The night before we left, when we were packing our suitcases, Cyndi was thinking and rethinking her selections. We both pack light—we often have the least luggage in the band—so we must make specific choices about clothing.

Cyndi held up a handful of clothes and looked at me for my opinion. "Should I take these instead?"

I started singing, "Don't go changing to try to please me, I love you just the way you are."

And then it occurred to me: we've done nothing but change for each other for the past forty years. Sorry, Billy Joel, but it's a silly song. Successful marriages are about constant change. Even after all these years, all I want to do is please Cyndi.

♦ ♦ ♦ ♦ ♦

I recently stuck this question on a shelf in my closet: "I wonder what my life would be like if I started doing all the things I'm afraid to do?" Surprisingly, the first thing I thought of was music.

One of my goals for 2017 was "to practice trombone at home more often," knowing that any practice at all, even only one time, would exceed what I'd been doing. But I needed more—a new, big goal to follow. It was time to reboot some ancient habits. So, I did something I'd been afraid to do. I signed up for private trombone lessons, my first since 1976.

"Why take private lessons at your age?" you might ask. "Don't you usually run away from situations where you appear to be a beginner? Isn't that the very thing you've been afraid of?"

Yes.

I knew taking lessons would be scary at first, exposing my fading ability to a professional musician who was probably younger than my son or daughter. But I hoped the scariness would last only one or two lessons, and then the constructive work would begin.

I'd grown lazy and complacent as a musician and needed a professional reboot. I was looking forward to starting over with basic exercises, happy to be reengaging with something I've loved since I was twelve. I was glad to know I still have improvement ahead of me.

The underlying reason I started taking lessons was this: I wanted to learn how to play improvisational jazz solos. It is on my list of "One Hundred Life Goals," and I had delayed getting started long enough. I've played in jazz bands since the beginning, but always as a section player. I was never brave enough to stand up and play a solo. And then, for some reason, in the fall of 2017 I decided my Fear of Looking Foolish (FOLF) was less than my Fear of Missing Out (FOMO). I didn't want to live out my life having never tried.

I'm so happy that playing trombone is still part of my life after all these years. I'm a better engineer because I'm a musician. I'm a better writer, a better teacher, a better husband, father, and lover. Having music in my life makes me creative, open-eyed, and helps me appreciate quality, hard work, and practice.

First Corinthians 1:5 says, "[God] has enriched your whole lives, from the words on your lips to the understanding in your hearts" (Phillips). Music is one of the most enriching gifts God has given me.

And it's one that is firmly embedded in my family. Dad was a church worship leader, and Mom played piano, so there was always music in our house. I was often "recruited" to play trombone solos in church, and since there weren't many soloists in those small congregations, I stayed in the regular rotation.

What's more, Cyndi and I first met in a band hall in 1973, and we've played in various ensembles together ever since. I cannot imagine our life without this bond between us.

One of my favorite Bible verses is Psalm 33:3, "Sing to [the Lord] a new song; play skillfully, and shout for joy." That's what it takes: skill (hard work) and joy (sheer pleasure). Or as my musical mentor and trail guide, Rabon, says, "You've got to dig what you're doing."

♦ ♦ ♦ ♦ ♦

I've tried to think my way into jazz for too many years. I assumed the way to learn to improvise would be to learn all the blues and jazz scales, maybe learn some cool licks in every key, and then good music would simply flow out of me. It was an intellectual and structured approach. Engineer-like, like me.

Nowadays I'm trying not to think so much, just listen and play. I'm not doing anything interesting yet, but it is fun to try. And I know it isn't enough to poke around in my practice room by myself. I must step out and play in front of people who know the difference.

I mentioned once to Rabon, "I suppose I have to commit to failing in front of my favorite people for at least a hundred times."

Rabon said, "Or a thousand times."

When I mentioned this to Bob, another jazz musician friend, he said, "You have to commit to failing every single time. You have to jump in all the way."

The thing is, this whole episode of my life is about more than just practicing, or learning different scales, or whatever. It's a deliberate move to receive guidance and encouragement from an expert, something adults don't get very often.

I like being told what to do.

I can't believe I just wrote that because I usually blow up when someone tells me what to do, but I suppose I have areas in my life where I appreciate it.

I like being coached when lifting weights or doing Pilates or yoga. I don't always want to decide on my own. And I like it when my trombone teacher, Ethan, shows me new software apps or new music or practice books. There is comfort in being directed, nurtured, and guided, especially when there is a mutual expectation that I will get much better.

My jazz sensei, Rabon, introduced me to a classic musical textbook by Madeline Bruser titled The Art of Practicing. In it she wrote, "Fear is energy. If you allow it to flow through you, you transform it into fearlessness. ... Each time you confront fear head on and let the adrenaline flood your body, you liberate the energy of fear and make it available for creative action."[23]

I've made a mental commitment, when playing with our local community college jazz band, to agree to take as many solos as possible and appropriate. I choose to be brave enough to stand up and play despite the fear of failing, looking and sounding like a beginner.

I know I'll get better with practice, but I need to practice in front of people. I must force the fear, take it on, and push through that barrier in order to improve and really learn. This is one of those things I cannot get better at by reading and studying. I have to clock in the time.

Karen Rinaldi wrote an interesting book called (It's Great to) Suck at Something. I'll admit I was hesitant to read it since sucking at something was what I was trying to avoid, but after I heard a podcast interview by the author, I decided to give it a try.

Rinaldi explains how working at something we aren't good at and will never be exceptional at leads to other opportunities and other situations that would never be possible otherwise, let alone on our personal radar, on our bucket list, under our consideration. She asks us to trust that working hard at this will bring results we can't imagine. Failing is often the only way to get better.

She writes that the ability to suck at something—which is weird to think of as an ability—is a learned skill. Most of the time, most of us won't even attempt something we don't think we can do well; we're more afraid of looking silly than of missing out. So yes, allowing ourselves to be bad in public is indeed an ability.

◆ ◆ ◆ ◆ ◆

I dreamed I was sitting inside a band hall full of chairs and music stands scattered randomly, like all band halls between rehearsals. I was the only musician in the room, and I was holding my trombone and sitting in the third chair from the end of the row when I heard a sharp rapping sound known to all musicians: the conductor calling his group to attention.

It seemed a little strange to me since I was apparently alone in the room, but I put my horn up out of habit and prepared to play. I didn't even have any music.

The Conductor said, "Let's begin."

"Begin what? I don't have any music."

"Just follow me and it'll be fine."

"Follow where? What do you want me to play?"

"Just follow my lead. Start in A-flat and try to keep up through the changes in the chorus."

"You want me to improvise in the key of A-flat? That means I have to play in fifth position. Nobody plays fifth in tune on a trombone. Let's do something else."

"You always want to do something else, don't you? You always want to pick the music yourself. I'm the conductor. Just follow me. Trust me."

"I do trust you. I just want to you to pick a key I can play well. How about something in F? I always play better in F."

"Not as often as you think."

"What? How often do you hear me play?"

"Well, I'm the one who gave you that horn. I'm the one who gave you music."

"My parents gave me this horn back in 1970."

"But I put music in your heart. It's because of me that you still play. And, by the way, it wouldn't have hurt if you'd have practiced a little more through the years."

"You wanted me to practice?"

"I gave you a gift; don't you think I expected you to practice a little?"

"Well, I did practice. I made All State, I played in college, I play in church orchestra—"

"I gave you a gift, and I wanted you to use it more often. But that is beside the point. Let's play!"

"I don't have any music."

"Improvise."

"You want me to play jazz?"

"Why do you always want a plan, a direction, a piece of music to look at? Is it so you won't have to follow me? You don't want to be a musician; you want to be a technician—a plan follower. I want you to follow me."

"OK, I'm ready. Should we tune?"

"Oh, suddenly you want to tune. All these years you didn't worry that much about tuning. You just wanted to play the notes."

"Should we tune?"

"We'll tune as we go. You're playing a trombone, the easiest instrument to play in tune. Remember, you're holding your tuning slide in your hand."

"Yeah, yeah, I've heard that my whole life from every band director I've known. If I'm holding my tuning slide in my hand, it also means a trombone is the easiest instrument to play out of tune."

"Don't get me started. You wanted choices. You wanted free will. You wanted to be independent. You could've played an instrument with structure and no obligation for tuning . . . like the triangle."

"But I'd only get to play one note."

"Do you want freedom or not? If you want to play a lot of notes, play them in tune. Let's go."

"Well, I'm sorry I've played out of tune so often. My ear isn't as good as it used to be."

"Your ear was never that good. Maybe if you'd practiced more . . ."

"The thing is, I can usually tell when I'm out of tune. I just can't tell if I'm sharp or flat. I can tell I'm off; I just don't know how to fix it."

"That's the smartest thing you've said since we started. You play the horn and let me tune for you as we go."

"You can tune my horn while I'm playing?"

"I don't care about your horn. I'll tune your heart. You just play."

"How will tuning my heart make me play well?"

"Stop worrying about whether you play well. That's my problem. All I want you to do is practice, and play, and listen, and follow me."

"So, what's my job again?"

"Follow me and let me tune your heart as we go."

"OK. So, what are we playing?"

"Just follow me."

Part Four

Staying CULTURALLY RELEVANT

Chapter 13

Not On My Own

Many carry the misconception that we should become more comfortable and that things should become easier as time goes by. This is a belief system designed to undermine you.

—Twyla Tharp

I was walking across the parking lot one Sunday morning after church, trying to find the best stride length and foot roll and posture to keep me from limping due to pain in my left ankle, the result of fallen arches and resulting ankle collapse.

I haven't had arches as far back as I can remember—by which I mean that I have very flat feet. I never paid attention to them until 1978, when I was shopping for my first pair of running shoes and reading articles about support, cushion, pronation, and the wet-foot-on-the-floor test to analyze the types of arches I had. When I stepped away from my own wet footprint, all I saw were parallel lines. No evidence of an arch at all, just flat feet. But my feet didn't bother me through nine marathons and all the training miles.

Until lately.

Maybe my once-crooked arthritic knees caused my ankles to shift inward. In any case, now that my legs are straighter and my knees don't hurt, my ankles have weakened, the tendons have shortened, and the bones have rearranged.

Twyla Tharp writes about "the significance of that final moment when your body breaks its contract with you."[24] That's what it felt like. A long-standing agreement had broken.

While walking across the parking lot, it occurred to me that from now on, my life would be a process of solving the weakest link one body issue at a time. My knees don't cause trouble nowadays. My right shoulder, while not as good as it originally was, is better and functional for almost anything I want to do. My current weakest links are my arches and ankles.

♦ ♦ ♦ ♦ ♦

When I heard Cyndi gasp, I was hoping she'd finally noticed my sculpted quads, but no, she was reacting to my feet. They weren't doing well. My arches, such as they were, had dropped, and my ankle bones were tilting inward. She wasn't proud, as I'd hoped, but worried.

My feet seem to be entering a new chapter of life, a common story with all the rest of my body parts since turning sixty. Pieces wilt and skills crash regularly. I've had to do more research and relearning to keep up and keep moving.

At the time of Cyndi's gasp, I was in her studio where she was thrashing me on a Pilates reformer machine under the guise of developing her teaching skills. She usually takes an obtuse direction when trying to change my life, knowing how I stubborn-up when confronted directly, but this time there was nothing subtle in her approach. She took charge and set me up with Chris, one of her yoga patrons, an experienced physical therapist and fellow cyclist. Chris wrapped my feet with about one hundred feet of tape and showed me how to do it myself. She was great, and my feet felt better right away when I walked around.

Chris also suggested arch supports for all my shoes. "Start small and work your way up. It takes time to retrain muscles and bones," she said.

I started taping and arch-supporting right away, satisfied with my progress and process. I'm always happier when I have a diagnosis and a plan.

That is, I was happy until I decided to replace the tape, which was looking gnarly and ragged. As I pulled it off, I noticed I'd pulled skin off, too. And I even had one blister on my heel. I hadn't noticed the damage before, and none of it hurt until I saw it. Then the pain started.

While I inspected for more damage, I noticed a series of deep blisters on the bottom of both feet, apparently from the overly ambitious arch supports I had been using.

Around our house I've often been accused of trying to do too much too soon, of thinking the regular rules don't apply to me and I can do things my own way. In this case I was trying to repair something quickly that had taken a lifetime to develop. I was too aggressive with tape and arch supports, and my feet paid the price.

Cyndi, who still hadn't caught her breath from that first glance at my ankles in the Pilates room, was nice about it this time. She even showed appropriate sympathy and concern over my plight.

So I decided to leave my feet alone long enough for the skin to heal and the blisters to calm down. The pause would give me a few days to ponder my habit of solving everything myself, often to my own discomfort.

Then one Thursday morning when I planned to leave town for the weekend, I felt a hard knot under the ball of my right foot. I thought, What have I done to make this even worse? I sat down and looked closely at my foot. A penny was stuck to the skin. The good news: my new problem was imaginary. The bad news: I had already started making plans for a new round of treatment. Sometimes I'm so smart, so intentional, so in-tune, I trick myself and make a mess.

A close friend once warned me about my tendency to solve problems using my own strength of will. Gary said, "Berry, you have the ability to figure out what has to happen, and that's where you have to be really careful. Because you can figure things out, there is a tendency to place God in the situation out of courtesy, but he doesn't really need to be there." I wasn't sure what he meant at the time, but in the years following, I've seen his warning play out in my life over and over. Too often I assume I can solve my problems on my own.

A week after pulling off the tape and skin, and three weeks after first frightening Cyndi, I was ready to start over. I told Cyndi, "It's time to resume treatment. I'll be more patient this time."

"I love you, Berry," she said, even with the we'll-see-about-that look in her eyes

◆ ◆ ◆ ◆ ◆

I ended my run one morning with an irritation on the right side of my right foot, midfoot. I thought it would be a blister, but when I looked, it was a small cut, or tear, or crack in the skin, running perpendicular to the long-axis of my foot.

It must have formed while my feet were taped, but I didn't notice until that morning. I had taken the tape off both feet the night before, after one and a half weeks of wearing it, to let them breathe. The skin on my right foot was flaky and crackly all over. And my left foot, not to miss out on the fun, developed an ache in the ankle at the level of the protruding bone. It changes my gait to a limp, but it doesn't show up every day nor worsen if I walk on it a lot. No doubt it's related to my arches and feet.

In fact, a week later, my massage magician, Bill, spent a lot of time working on my ankle and surrounding tendons. He said that because of the fallen arches, the tendons on the inside were stretched and the tendons on the outside were tight and hardened from sixty years. And the injury had crept upward toward my ankle.

Bill said, "When you have as much tenure as we do, you have to respond in new ways."

So I've been doing toe exercises and toe lifts during the day. Sometimes I take off my shoes at work and walk around my office in my socks, hoping to strengthen my feet. A foam roller ball kept under my desk lets me roll my feet and ankles in all directions while sitting and working. There's also the Pilates strength training I do with Cyndi once a week. My feet limit my number of reps, but hopefully the Pilates will help strengthen them and maybe even rearrange my arches.

♦ ♦ ♦ ♦ ♦

I couldn't sleep Wednesday night because my foot was aching. It scared me. Back when my knees were at their worst, I knew there was a permanent solution available: joint replacement. With my ankles and feet, I'm not so sure.

I once lost a city-wide election that I was certain God had told me to pursue. Only later did I realize I needed to leave government, to clear my calendar, to clear my life for the next set of adventures. Had I simply left office on my own, I might have wondered forever if I quit too soon. But losing an election was final. Is that what this foot problem is about? Is God clearing my calendar and life for the next thing?

Lying in bed, holding Cyndi's hand for confidence, softly so I wouldn't wake her, I prayed a three-part prayer: God, please heal my feet. Show me what to do to make them better. And change my heart to prepare me for whatever comes next.

The next morning, the first thought across my mind was to visit Smith's Shoes in Odessa ("Engineering Comfort Since 1975"). When I pray for guidance, I feel obligated to act on the first thoughts that cross my mind. Otherwise, why waste time praying?

I texted Cyndi to tell her I was driving over for Smith's advice and help that afternoon. Cyndi wanted to go with me, which made me happy. I always like it when she's with me, and even more when I'm nervous about my own future. I need her endorsement and her approval to push forward into new things.

I bought a pair of casual Brooks trainers and a pair of office-appropriate New Balances, and I had custom orthotics fitted to my feet for both pairs of shoes. Maybe this won't completely solve my problems, but I always feel better when I have a plan of action and take positive steps toward a solution.

It seems we are always doing at least one of three things: training (to get better and stronger); rehabilitating (to recover and mend damage); or compensating (to accommodate an injury in order to keep moving, as in using props in yoga class to make up for lost flexibility.)

My friend Clark pointed out a fourth thing: sometimes we surrender.

♦ ♦ ♦ ♦ ♦

Cyndi and I have been making plans to hike on the Camino in Spain this May. We've talked around the idea for years and finally decided it was time to go. It's the most pressing reason I am nervous about my feet. I want to be healthy enough and fit enough to do it.

Two weeks ago, we were skiing in Santa Fe with our family, including granddaughters, and I had to limit my runs to protect my left ankle. I changed boots the second day to accommodate my ankle, and it seemed to help. It certainly gave me more confidence.

When we got back home to Midland, Cyndi asked how I felt. She knew I was worried. "How do you feel about going forward? Will you ski again?"

"I hope so. I'm not ready to start quitting things yet. But I don't know if this is an outlier or a trend I have to surrender to."

"You know you don't have to figure it out on your own."

"Thanks."

Chapter 14

A Less Busy Heart

Friday was our day in Jerusalem to visit the Western Wall, and we began by going underground. Our tour guide asked if anyone was catastrophobic (an accidental portmanteau from *catastrophe* and *claustrophobic*). He asked because we were going into our second tunnel tour in two days.

Most of the old archeological sites in Jerusalem are deep under the city, and tunnels are how they were discovered and explored. This particular tunnel followed the length of the Western Wall.

After the temple was destroyed by the Romans in 70 CE, the bases of the walls were covered in rubble. Succeeding conquests continued to fill in the valley to make the city easier to defend and make more space for houses, which means that today, much of the Western Wall extends dozens of feet below ground level. So the tunnels were excavated to trace the wall and understand the generations of development around it.

After an hour in the tunnel, we went to the above-ground part of the Western Wall where Jews go to pray because it is the closest they can get to the location of the Holy of Holies in the Second Temple. Our guide gave us some time to take photos, observe, and pray.

Not wanting to cause an international incident, and not certain of rules or protocol, I approached the portion of the wall not occupied by the tribe of men dressed in all black, with big black hats, who were swaying forward and backward as they prayed. I went south of them to a spot where there were more men dressed like me.

I found a tiny crack between stones and inserted my piece of paper with this simple prayer: Jesus, make your home in my heart; make me like you.

I stood for a few minutes with both hands on the wall, absorbing the energy from two thousand years of accumulated prayers with my entire body, before retreating back to a white plastic chair (they were scattered all over). I wanted to soak in the environment, let God speak to me through this.

There is a part of me that wants the attention to detail, the focus, the physical connection I saw in the worshipers around me. It's so easy for me to descend into an intellectual understanding of faith. I need more physical, tangible connections to ground me in reality.

♦ ♦ ♦ ♦ ♦

"I'm going to walk" was the first thing I said to a quiet room and a sleeping Cyndi one morning in Midland. I was still prone in bed, but my inclination was in the direction of getting up. It was 6:20 a.m. and I had been lying in bed arguing with myself whether to roust myself and walk around the neighborhood pond since my alarm first went off at six. Unfortunately, I've become adept at turning it off and going back to sleep.

But this time I did the right thing. I got up, pulled on gym shorts, T-shirt, and Hokas, waited while Cyndi got dressed (she hadn't been thinking about it for twenty minutes like I had), and we did our morning walk.

Our neighborhood has a beautiful private park created by the developers, who turned a drainage project into one of the coolest places in Midland. It has two ponds, lots of trees, and even a small man-made bubbling stream. The walking path is one mile long if you circle both ponds, and this morning it had a Disneyesque quality about it: birds singing, ducks quacking, bunnies hopping, and fish flopping.

When we first moved into this neighborhood, we had an aging Labrador named Lady, and we walked her around the pond twice a day. In her long life with us, over twelve years, Lady ran thousands of miles with Cyndi early in the morning before sunrise and me in the evening after work. By the time we moved here in 2008, Lady was too old and creaky to run long with us, so we walked her though the park every morning and evening.

Because I was tethered to Lady by the leash, I couldn't go any faster than she did, so I was forced to slow down. Those slow walks through the park became a meditative, prayerful experience.

Now, without Lady, there is no reason I can't cross the street by myself and pray as I walk. But without the responsibility of having a dog to walk, I never get around to it.

Last fall Cyndi and I started getting up at 6:00 a.m. to walk the ponds, and we had several successful streaks of daily trips. But something inevitably interrupted our schedule, and the pattern would go dormant for weeks. Or months. This morning, we resisted the resistance and took our walk.

I believe in the magic of daily practices that take me inside myself, allow my thoughts to wander, and allow my heart to be open and vulnerable. Walking the ponds was once a daily practice of mine, and I wanted it back.

But first I needed the discipline to get up and do it, day after day. Deep spiritual practices start out as chores. It takes a lot of reps to convert ideas into habits into practices.

In his book Soul Keeping, John Ortberg wrote, "Prayer, meditation, and confession actually have the power to rewire the brain in a way that can make us less self-referential and more aware of how God sees us."[25] That is my strongest motivation for daily practices, and my greatest expectation—to let God rewire my brain.

It's like those phone apps that ask permission to access my location, and I have to agree if I want to use the app, knowing that the app will use the data for its own purpose. When I pray, when I meditate, when I practice daily, I'm opening myself to God, giving him my password, giving him permission to access my ideas and thoughts and dreams and loves and goals, and asking him to manipulate those to his pleasure.

♦ ♦ ♦ ♦ ♦

My prayer practice has become more frequent, richer, deeper, and more personal as I've gotten older. I pray more often, especially lots of short prayers all through the day.

I've never been much of a public prayer. I have prayed aloud at my church many times, and I pray at the close of each of my Bible classes. But I was never good about family prayer devotions, and I tend to avoid prayer meetings. I'm not sure why, but they never pull me in and I never feel comfortable. I spend the entire time wondering how much longer this is going to last.

For me, prayer is the hardest spiritual discipline to wrap my thoughts around. While I understand the importance of prayer and the value of prayer, not to mention the obedience of prayer, and in fact I enjoy prayer, it's hard for me to know what to pray for.

But there's the nub: "what to pray for." If the only reason we come to God in prayer is to get stuff, or make things happen, we're missing the most important part. Prayer teaches us what God is like and, in fact, teaches us what we are like. Through the process of discovering God's character and our own character, we grow more and more like him. As we do, our will conforms to his will, and we find ourselves praying increasingly in God's will—not because we got lucky enough to land on it but because we have become more like God.

In A Praying Life, Paul Miller wrote, "Learning to pray doesn't offer us a less busy life; it offers us a less busy heart."[26] I want a less busy heart. That should be reason enough to pray.

♦ ♦ ♦ ♦ ♦

I often tell God, "This is the path I plan to take. It feels good to me right now, so I'll probably stay on this direction unless you disrupt me by changing my heart and mind or putting an obstacle in my way. I'm not asking you to endorse my plans, but I am asking you to intervene and change me if I need something else." I don't know how to be any more honest than that.

♦ ♦ ♦ ♦ ♦

During one of my trips to Santa Fe, I found myself in the Cathedral Basilica of St. Francis. I wanted to sit there a while. To my left was a statue of the Virgin Mary called La Conquistadora, which first arrived at this location in 1626. The current cathedral was completed and dedicated in 1887, and most of its statues were a mystery to me. Catholicism is not the tradition that raised me. My life has been firmly Protestant and Baptist, traditions that shy away from icons. I wonder if we're as noble as we think we are in that regard.

I like to come to this cathedral and be still, to feel the space, to soak in the silence, to slow down and let my brain floaters settle, and to listen and absorb the centuries of worship. Even though my own tradition and theology is significantly different from what is represented here, the object of our worship is the same for me as for the generations who've sat here before me.

I often wonder if we modern evangelicals put too much effort into making our worship centers as nonreligious as possible, with industrial-grade, flat-black ceilings, offering no incentive to tilt our heads and follow the columns and vaults as they point upward. We miss the nobility of architecture that draws worshiper's eyes and hearts toward heaven.

As much as I lean into the future, which is a core value for me, my spirit longs to tap into the ancient streams of faith, to follow the footsteps of generations, to feel the strength and power flowing through all those who've come before—to, as Aslan said, experience "a magic deeper still,"[27] to sing what my friend Matthew Clark has called "an anthem born before the world began."

Richard Rohr teaches that change and growth must be programmed into our spirituality or we'll end up worshiping the status quo. My hope is to disrupt daily patterns and open my heart to a fresh word from God, whether that means being physically still and quiet in a large space steeped in history or pushing myself up a hill on an unfamiliar road.

♦ ♦ ♦ ♦ ♦

I was eating lunch at McDonald's when a young mother with two kids sat beside me. The youngsters sat patiently (I was surprised) while their mom got their food and drinks. She put three drink cups with plastic lids and straws on the table. The girl, about eight, looked at the lid to see which plastic "bubble" was pushed down, indicating which drink was hers. "This one says diet," she said, and handed the drink to her mother. She read the next lid and said proudly, "This one says cola—it must be for me."

The little boy, about four, was tired of his big sister being in charge again, so he grabbed the remaining cup, looked at the lid, and said loudly, "This one says MINE!"

It was a good description of my basic prayer life so far. I can pray for other people and say, "Here, this is for you," but when I start praying about my own life I pull back and say loudly, "This one is mine."

In his book With Open Hands, Henri Nouwen described the act of prayer as opening our hands to God.[28] Opening up and releasing our grip on fears and dreams and our own perfect plan for our own perfect lives. It also means opening up and being ready to receive whatever God has to offer.

Learning to do as Nouwen suggested—praying with open hands—may take me awhile to learn.

How can I stand in surrender to God? How can I truly pray with open hands, ready to give all and ready to receive all? Can

I open my hands before I know what God wants me to give up? Can I open my hands before I know what he wants to give me in return?

Surrender would be easier if I knew the terms beforehand. Like General Robert E. Lee at Appomattox, I want to know if my army can keep their sidearms and horses before I hand over my sword and sign the papers. I want a picture of what my life will be after I surrender before I actually surrender.

Nouwen said that to open my hands is an admission that I am not God, that I am through trying to be God, and that I was not particularly good at it anyway. Opening my hands is an admission that I am better off trusting the mysterious and unknown will of God than trusting my own ability to maneuver through life. It's harder than it sounds, though, because it makes me vulnerable. What if I'm not prepared for what God has for me? What if God puts me in some position that's over my head and beyond my abilities? What if God puts me in so deep my own self isn't good enough? What if God puts me into a life I cannot live without trusting in him?

It is hard for me to accept that a life in God's hands could be better than a life in my own hands. My own dreams for life are pretty good: Cyndi and I get to do what we want and travel whenever and wherever we want; all our kids are smiling and happy, successful, and honoring God with their lives; I am running sub-three-hour marathons regularly and reading and writing all the time; and everyone around us is walking with God because of the tremendous impact we have had on their lives. What is wrong with a dream like that, I ask?

The thing is, I have no reason to be afraid of God's plans for my life. When I look at my life so far—and especially if I am holding Cyndi's hand as I look—I see nothing but wonderful blessings from God. Why am I afraid to release my own dreams, open my hands to God, and rest in his care?

The tighter I hold on, the less I can receive. If I keep my hands clinched around my own dreams and ideas, I can't catch what God has to offer. If I want to receive God's blessings, I must open my hands to accept, and that means letting go of my tight grip.

I guess that after all these years as a believer, I still have a lot of growing up to do. I'm in the adolescent stage of my Christian walk, concerned with what I want without any accompanying responsibility or obligation. Like a teenager, I just want God's blessings handed to me at no cost to myself.

The good news is, according to Nouwen, I can learn to surrender to God a little at a time. Daily prayer may be the best way to grow out of spiritual youth and into adulthood. Daily praying with open hands.

Chapter 15

Keep Exploring

Turning sixty was liberating. I got a new stack of blank pages ready to fill with promises, possibilities, mysteries, and adventures. I had a new chance at life. Old things passed away; new things were coming. I was finally old enough to grow my hair out again, like I did in the 1970s, like a Hogwarts headmaster, or better, like Zorro (Anthony Hopkins edition).

When I turned fifty, it felt like release. I said goodbye to all expectations of being cool or hip or fashionable and started crediting my idiosyncrasies as eccentricities. It was great. I was finally living up to my gray hair and beard.

No one, including me, cared if I knew current pop songs or TV shows. In fact, even better, no one expected me to know. It was grand.

When I turned forty, I finally felt like an adult. (No, that's not entirely correct. Even today I only feel like an adult about 50 to 60 percent of the time. I always think of adults as the men of my dad's generation, whatever age that happens to be.) However, by forty, I could no longer hide behind my age. I was old enough to know stuff, old enough to stop blaming behavior on my upbringing, old enough to formulate my own opinions without basing them on a talk radio host or what the guys at work say, old enough to settle into my reading list and read the books I enjoy, old enough to learn new ideas, old enough to change my mind.

When I turned thirty, well, that one is still a blur in my memory. We had a six-year-old and a three-year-old, and dadhood took its toll on my brain cells. The summer of my birthday we moved but didn't move to California, due to a promotion I got and then didn't get. A few months later I was with my son, Byron, when he was hit by a car while we were all riding bikes one Saturday afternoon. It changed my understanding of being a father and spiritual leader. I learned that bad things could happen to those I love even if I was acting responsibly and following the rules. It was the first time in my life when I called upon God out of desperation and fear.

The year I turned twenty was my last of three summers touring with the Continental Singers as a bass trombonist, and it was my segue into big-time college life at the University of Oklahoma. It was the beginning of my lifelong journey with personal discipleship, my introduction to daily spiritual practices and teaching, my first experience with leaders who deliberately invested in my life, and my first date with Cyndi Richardson. Little did I know I was starting the adventures that would define my future.

Recently my daughter, Katie, gave me a red-and-white patch that says, "Keep Exploring." In the 1970s I would've sewn it on my bell-bottom blue jeans so everyone else could see it, but instead I asked Cyndi to sew it on my backpack so I would see it every day as a permanent reminder of how I want to live.

The Keep Exploring movement was created by Alex and Bret, two young men from Flower Mound, Texas. In a blog post on their website, Alex writes, "Keep Exploring is the simple idea that adventure can be found anywhere. We are trying to be better explorers by seeking out opportunities in everyday life. This is a collaborative movement – Everyone is invited. Start looking for new roads to take, old mountains to climb, and wild food to chew."[29]

Well, that's who I want to be. Maybe not the chewing-of-wild-food part, but I want my sixties to be years of exploring new ideas, trails, mountains, techniques, books, movies, relationships, influences, and music.

One Sunday afternoon I was cycling with my friend Wes, and we were working through our increasing list of athletic ailments. Wes changed everything by saying, "This is the best time of our lives. We're finally old enough that people listen to us. We can really make a difference."

I thought about what he said for a long time. Through the years I've been motivated by this thought: If I apply the weight of my life toward the people God has entrusted to me, I can change the world. But now even that seems too small. I no longer want to merely change the world—I want to change The Future. I am finally old enough, finally weighty enough, to speak truth into hearts and change the future.

♦ ♦ ♦ ♦ ♦

What have I left behind in becoming an adult? Well, I've left behind the impatience and longing to be a grownup who can make his own decisions, do whatever he wants, and spend his own money. It turned out to be more about worry and obligation than wide-horizon freedom.

I've left behind excuses. Whatever adult skills I've yet to acquire, such as auto mechanics or golf, I can no longer say no one has taught me. Anything I don't know, or know how to do, is my own fault, and I have no one to blame but myself.

Another thing I've left behind is the idea I have to be good at everything. When I was young, I tried lots of things—soccer, racquetball, cycling, writing, politics, and on and on. Some of those turned out to be who I am, others I tossed over the side. It was a breakthrough for me when I realized I didn't have to keep doing whatever I started for the rest of life. I could change my mind and move on to something else. I look back on those young-adult days as my trial-and-error phase. Now I don't want to accumulate; I want to narrow and refine.

♦ ♦ ♦ ♦ ♦

It has occurred to me that when I use words like liberating (in my sixties) and release (in my fifties), it sounds like I might be disengaging, giving up, maybe even running away. But what I intend to do is engage—step up and lean forward. Liberating release is the freedom to be myself.

That sounds so high-minded, but the truth is, freedom is costly. Not everything about aging is a reward. The price is usually sudden and shocking and includes some loss of ability or function.

I recently told my friend Bill how the slightest bump can put brown bruises on my skin, and I quickly start bleeding. He was having the same problem. It was a recent phenomenon for both of us, a product of aging.

For example, I was in Best Buy entering the checkout line when a blue-shirted employee asked if I was OK. She was pointing at my arm, specifically at the trail of blood running across my skin. I had apparently bumped my arm on one of the display racks as I circled the checkout maze, a bump so slight I didn't notice, but now I was bleeding. This sort of thing happens way too often. I never expected my hands to turn into my dad's hands. I'm not happy about that.

Bill and I wondered if all the fanny packs worn by men in the retirement village where my dad used to live, the ones I thought were full of snacks and candy, were really full of body repair kits: Band-Aids, Liquid Skin, Super Glue, Ace Bandages, Advil, absorbent towels, and so on. Was that our future?

I don't resent the effects of aging. I just want to know how to deal with them, how to do workarounds, how to compensate and keep moving. I suppose I could stay home and sit in my recliner, where it's safe. But as Jeff, my friend and eye doctor, once reminded me, "That's not a world you and I want to live in."

♦ ♦ ♦ ♦ ♦

Getting older reminds me of being a teenager. Remember how we were completely shocked that all our new freedoms and opportunities were accompanied by increased expectations and obligations? Every generation is stunned to learn they are now responsible to take care of themselves and take care of their own business when all they wanted was their own phone, their own truck, and a chance to stay up late.

In the same way, I'm constantly surprised at the new baggage that occupies my silver-haired years. One recent Saturday morning I woke up with a stiff and painful ankle. How could anyone sprain their ankle while sleeping?

Here's another: I've never had great vision—I was the kid in first grade wearing glasses—but I'm still surprised whenever I can't see. Just last night, feeling noble, I dug out my old Bible memory verse cards only to realize I couldn't read them. The writing was impossibly small. What was I thinking when I wrote them out so tiny? I don't know how I ever read those.

And now that I have finally outgrown face zits, which by the way took decades longer than I expected, I get blotches and bumps and tags on my face, all of which look like cancer to me. I even started going to a dermatologist. On my first visit he asked, "Mr. Simpson, what brought you in this morning?" I said, "I decided to be a grownup for a change and get professional advice." He told me my concerns were nothing more than marks of old age, and I should come back next year.

Yet, even with all these strange aging indicators—and I haven't mentioned them all since memory is a big one—I love the freedom and understanding that comes with age. I don't resent transitioning from running to cycling or adapting from tiny print to 12-point font. I wonder what will be next.

I fully expect the next years to be the best ones. I just read a headline that said, "'World's oldest backpacker' plans two-month trip to Europe at 95 years old."[30] That sounds great to me, like something I want to do. I hope my shoulder feels better by then.

♦ ♦ ♦ ♦ ♦

I'm typing this with Band-Aids on my right hand: one on my right thumb, and the other on my right index finger. They're the cloth-type Band-Aids, flexible and persistent, but they collect every speck of dirt that meanders by. After a few hours my hand feels like I'm wearing a bulky cotton work glove. It's a clumsy and awkward setup, and I don't recommend it. The inconvenience soon surpasses any pain from the original injury, and I am tempted to pull them off and try typing without them. It's only my years as a grown-up, which have taught me that healing takes time, that tell me to keep the Band-Aids in place.

What happened to my hand? One evening Cyndi and I joined the local bike club for the Urban Mountain Bike Ride. We don't get to ride together often, so this felt like a date. Instead of buying flowers, though, I bought Cyndi a front and back light for her bike. It was a great start.

After we arrived at the Midland College parking lot, I unloaded and reassembled the bikes and pedaled around a bit on each one to make sure everything worked. While I was riding my own bike and adjusting my helmet mirror, not paying attention to where I was going since it's a huge parking lot and what could possibly happen, I ran into one of those bright yellow curb bumpers. I didn't know I'd collided with the bumper until I hit the asphalt.

Fortunately for me, I was creeping along, so my crash didn't result in any road rash. However, I ended up with a cut in my thumb and finger, a knot on my right thigh, and a strangeness on my left hip.

I could tell right away these were only superficial wounds and wouldn't interfere with the fun of the evening. After shooing away all the potential first-aiders, I checked to make sure my bike wasn't damaged. Both wheels and brakes worked. I was ready to move.

As far as bike crashes go, this was mostly benign. Two Band-Aids and two days of sore quads and I was fine. Not like my 2013 crash, which left me with a watermelon-sized butt and hip and weekly visits to my hospital's wound management unit for the entire summer. This time it was inconvenience rather than real injury.

The morning after my crash, I told my story to a surprisingly unsympathetic friend who asked, "Aren't you too old to be hitting the pavement?"

"Yes, I am."

What I didn't tell my friend, who is someone who would never hit the pavement because they never do anything except sit on the couch and watch TV, was that there is risk with not doing Urban Mountain Bike Rides. The risk of losing adventure and heart and soul.

Still, my friend was correct: I'm too old to be hitting the pavement. While I hope to have many years of risk and adventure ahead, I'm old enough and smart enough to look where I'm going and wait to adjust my helmet mirror until I stop moving. Each adventure—each blank page, each phase of life—requires its own wisdom and responsibility.

♦ ♦ ♦ ♦ ♦

And then I woke up one Wednesday morning with a broken toe. At least, that's what it felt like.

The big toe on my left foot felt like I had jammed it, or broken it, sometime during the night while I was peacefully asleep in bed. That scenario seemed unlikely, but I couldn't deny the stiffness and swelling and pain. All my toes were puffed up like Vienna Sausages. Even worse, my middle toe was bright red, probably infected.

I hobbled around all day hoping I could bring the pain to submission though strength of will, my usual technique of self-medication, but I was unsuccessful. I just felt old and lame and helpless. This wasn't the sort of injury I could walk my way through. I was miserable.

Friday morning I went to see my doctor. The minute he walked into the room and saw my foot he said, "Well, there is obvious infection in that one toe. But your main problem is gout."

Bummer. Gout. One of the most ancient of diseases, documented as far back as 350 BC by Hippocrates himself. Now I really felt old.

The good news is, by Monday morning, six days after my flare-up, I seemed to be about 85 percent back to normal. I even walked the mile around our neighborhood ponds. On Wednesday I walked about three miles. Maybe the comeback trail is a real possibility?

Of course, none of my complaints surprise God. He's known all about me for a long time now. In fact, Psalm 139 says he planned each day of my life—he charted those days even before I was born. Every moment, he knows where I am, and he both precedes and follows me and places his hand of blessing on my head. Who could whine or complain about treatment like that?

♦ ♦ ♦ ♦ ♦

In the movie A Walk in the Woods, Bill Bryson (played by Robert Redford) was standing in line at a funeral, waiting to speak to the widow, when a friend in line behind him tapped him on the shoulder and said, "Makes you think of slowing down, doesn't it?"

I remember hearing that line in the movie theater. I almost stood up and said aloud, "No, it makes me want to speed up!"

♦ ♦ ♦ ♦ ♦

When I approached the one-year anniversary of my father's death, people asked how I was doing. And the truth: I was doing just fine. Dad died well. He left no accounts unsettled, whether financial, emotional, or family. He did what he loved best all the way to the end, cycling up to his last two weeks and cracking jokes up to his last five days.

Oliver Sacks wrote in his small but profound book Gratitude, "When my time comes, I hope I can die in harness, as Francis Crick did."[31] (Crick died at eighty-eight from colon cancer, still fully engaged in his most creative work all the way to the end.) I like this. Dying in harness sounds fun, adventurous, and fulfilling.

Sacks left me wondering what dying in harness would look like for me. Does it mean I might die . . .

. . . at my engineer desk, working on a problem, face pressed into my computer keyboard?

. . . at some Whataburger booth while writing in my journal? If so, I hope whatever I am writing is good and not stupid. I don't want people to think my writing became so incoherent I committed suicide in the restaurant rather than kept trying.

... on my bicycle? If so, I hope I have a heart attack and slip off into the barrow ditch, not get blown away by some big truck while the driver is texting. And I hope I'm flying with a tailwind so at least I'll be smiling.

... while hiking? That would be great. Of course, it might be days before they found my body, which could be unpleasant for the finders.

... while playing trombone? I usually play in public, so that would be traumatic. Especially if I keeled over while on stage at church.

... climbing the stairs in my office building? Again, it might be a long time before I was missed and even longer before I was located in a seldom-used stairwell. I suppose if they found my pickup abandoned in the parking garage, someone would think to look in the stairs.

... while teaching? It would be dramatic, that's for sure, and it might leave emotional scars on my class. I would hope to go out while making a significant point.

... while skiing? Crashing into a tree would be preferable to having a heart attack while riding the lift and leaving hundreds of people stranded while the ski patrol unloaded me from the chair.

Sacks also wrote about his own father, who lived to age ninety-four and who often said that "the eighties had been one of the most enjoyable decades of his life. He felt, as I begin to feel, not a shrinking but an enlargement of mental life and perspective."[32]

I recently opened my copy of Soul Salsa, by Leonard Sweet, to browse through it again. When I first read this book in 2005, I wrote some notes on the first page: "As I get older, I want to: lean forward not backward, be less dogmatic, default to grace, give away more money, time, energy, creativity, life, music, books, insight." I was pleased that none of those wishes had diminished in the fifteen years since I first wrote them.

Most developed-world countries have accepted the chronological age of sixty-five years as a definition of elderly. So, at the moment I am writing this, I have fifteen more months of middle age to enjoy.

The ability to change the future, and the freedom to keep exploring, comes with additional responsibility and obligation. The apostle Paul admonished in 2 Corinthians 8:11, "Now finish the work, so that your eager willingness to do it may be matched by your completion of it, according to your means." Maybe that is what staying "in harness" all the way to the end of life really means. We should stay engaged in the purpose and calling God has given us, finishing as strong as we began.

Part Five

A LIFELONG STUDENT of SIGNIFICANT THINGS

Chapter 16

Practicing Faith

My love for spiritual practices began when I was a junior at the University of Oklahoma. I fell in with a group of leaders and students at the Baptist Student Union who taught the value of spiritual practices. At the time, that for me meant Scripture memorization, Bible study, teaching, and group worship. It was what I needed to hear and do, so I joined right in.

As I got older my list expanded. To my surprise, running became a spiritual practice, even though spiritual pursuit had no bearing on why I started running in the beginning. It's as if God saw me doing something on a regular basis, in a systematic way, and decided to join me. In my new post-knee-replacement era, I'm walking instead of running; I expect walking will become a spiritual practice in the same way that running did, but only time will tell. Cycling too.

And my list of spiritual practices has continued to grow. Most of my hiking and backpacking is in pursuit of God. I expect to hear from him on the trail.

Writing has certainly become a spiritual practice for me, helping me learn what God is telling me, setting it in my life, allowing me to work out my theology and understanding. Writing also allows me to tell the stories and share the lessons I learn. It's in the telling that I see the real work of God.

I've learned that if I do the practices—read from my Bible every day, read spiritual books, pray, find time for solitude and searching, share and teach what I've learned, memorize and meditate, get around other believers and let them influence me, listen to good teaching and preaching, and all that—well, if I'm true to the practices, God speaks to me. Through constant practice, Christianity makes sense beyond my rational mind; it makes sense in my heart and soul.

Spiritual practices don't earn us an audience with God or mark us as serious disciples, but the process of repetition changes us, changes our heart, changes our motives, and changes our character to be more like Jesus. Spiritual practices don't attract God's attention; they focus our own attention toward God. They open our ears.

◆ ◆ ◆ ◆ ◆

The apostle Paul wrote, "I discipline body and make it my slave, so that, after I have preached to others, I myself will not be disqualified."[33]

What specifically did Paul mean when he said he disciplined his body? I doubt Paul went to weightlifting classes. Was he a runner? He certainly referenced running often in his writing. He also mentioned boxing; do you think he was into boxing? The New Living Translation renders the same verse as, "I discipline my body like an athlete, training it to do what it should."

We don't know what disciplines Paul engaged in, but he was a man who believed in spiritual practices.

But even more mysterious than Paul's workout discipline is this: What did he mean that he could be disqualified?

Disqualified from what? Preaching? Writing? Traveling? Mentoring? Was he afraid he might lose his turn, or that people would stop listening to him, or that maybe he'd die too soon?

It's unsettling to think that I could be disqualified from teaching because of the way I take care of my physical body. I don't want to be disqualified because I was too soft or too lazy to treat my body like an athlete, training it to do what it should. So, I keep practicing.

♦ ♦ ♦ ♦ ♦

There is a Bible story about a young man named Daniel who got into Trouble. Not just trouble with a small t, but Trouble, condemned to death in a den of lions for praying to God rather than worshiping the Babylonian king. Daniel wasn't being momentarily rebellious, not making some grand political gesture. He was just doing what he did every day, simply because that's what he did—his consistent, daily practice that gave him strength for life. And God rewarded him for it with wisdom and strong faith. Daniel survived not only the lion's den but also a lifetime living in a pagan and hostile regime without losing his love for God or compromising his faith.

In the margin of my Bible, I wrote about another young man, one I knew personally, who said he wanted to grow deeper with God, but he wasn't interested in hearing about the same old quiet time or any of that. I remember thinking at the time, knowing the truth but not sure how to express it, that it was repeated, daily practice that would take him deeper, not some sort of special insight or cool worship experience. For him it might not be a traditional quiet time, but he needed something that he repeated day after day after day.

Like Daniel in the window.

♦ ♦ ♦ ♦ ♦

One of the first Bible verses I learned, more than thirty years ago, was 2 Corinthians 5:17: "If anyone is in Christ, he is a new creature; the old things passed away; behold, new things have come" (NASB). I quoted that verse to myself for years, expecting that my old things were passing away, replaced by new things.

Then one day in 1978, as I walked across the campus at the University of Oklahoma, between a petroleum fluids class and an economics lecture, it occurred to me that I didn't understand that verse at all. (It usually happens to me that way: a sudden realization that I'm not as smart as I thought. It's always a disappointment.)

I did a quick assessment of my life and realized that the passing of old and replacement by new wasn't so automatic or complete as I'd thought. Apparently, I needed to take a more active part. Maybe the verse meant that God had given me permission to change, or the ability to change, or the grace to change, but I certainly hadn't become a new person by osmosis.

If I wanted those new things to come—things like love, joy, peace, patience, kindness, goodness, gentleness, faithfulness, self-control—I had to discipline myself and practice them.

However, I didn't know how to practice peace or kindness. They seemed to be more by-products of a disciplined life than actual habits I could learn. I decided to focus on things I could learn.

It was a relief, actually. I understood prayer, daily reading, meditation, memorizing, attending worship, and fasting. They were tangible. I could plan them into my life. I believed my motives would eventually change if I kept at it long enough. I also expected to grow in love and joy and gentleness.

Phillip Yancey wrote about becoming godlike: "I wish the process were spontaneous and natural, but I have never found it so. Indeed, I have found that such a process, like anything of worth, requires discipline."[34] I agreed with him; I kept practicing.

As it turned out, most of the things I do in life that I'm good at . . . well, they've happened because I've practiced so hard. For example, I've spent hours practicing writing, reading books, and attending writers' workshops. Why? Because I want to get better. I need the practice.

It's the same with teaching. I work hard at being a good teacher. I run my ideas past Cyndi, who is the best teacher I know, and I'm constantly analyzing and reevaluating what worked and what didn't. I want to get better.

I guess you could say the same thing about running, except that running is a different category. While I believe I had a beginning level of talent as a writer and teacher, I had absolutely no natural talent or ability as a runner other than perseverance. I run nowadays not because I've gotten better but because once I started, I never quit. I just didn't stop. Through the years I've practiced continually (we usually call it training) by doing speed work at the track, and long runs on the weekends, and occasional stadium-step workouts. I've done that since 1978, but when I look back at my old logbooks, it's clear that I haven't improved more than 5–10 percent since I started. I don't have much success to show for all that practice.

But I still try because I know the daily discipline of running has changed my life in more profound ways than merely lowering my marathon times.

Which brings me back to practicing spiritual disciplines. We shouldn't practice just the things we are good at. Some of us may have a natural talent for memorizing Scripture, and with practice we could become powerful lions of the Word. Others of us have no natural talent at it, and twenty-five years of daily practice will yield only marginal improvement. But in either case, the daily discipline will change us in ways we cannot measure and maybe cannot even perceive. If we just keep practicing the things of God, our old things will pass away, and day by day, new things will come.

♦ ♦ ♦ ♦ ♦

A Spirit-led life is about incremental changes over a lifetime. Those changes can be permanent and can ripple out to the lives surrounding us. As Mark Batterson wrote, "Make no mistake about it, those spiritual disciplines accrue compound interest."[35]

♦ ♦ ♦ ♦ ♦

I once had a leather portfolio that had belonged to Cyndi's grandfather, Forrest Atchley. Someone in the family gave it to me after Forrest died. I think it was Aunt Teena. It was old and stiff, having laid on a shelf for years, maybe decades, but I wanted to use it. If the entire portfolio couldn't be salvaged, I wanted to use the leather to make a cover for my Daily Bible. I took it to a leather shop, and they tried but told me there was too much dry rot. It could not be saved. There were no parts of it large enough to use.

It had dried up out of non-use.

♦ ♦ ♦ ♦ ♦

So many people want to be a marathon runner but don't want to make room in their daily schedule to run.

They want to be a cyclist in Texas but are afraid to ride in the heat and complain about the wind.

They want to be a jazz musician but can't find five minutes a day for practice.

They want to be a flatbelly but won't do any ab workouts or make the effort to eat less.

They want to be a best-selling author but won't bother with marketing.

They want to be the noun without doing the verb.

♦ ♦ ♦ ♦ ♦

David Brooks wrote about his life after converting to Christianity. "I'd had many Christian friends, but now I was asking them a bit more about how they lived. I learned about the spiritual disciplines and concepts that formed their daily and annual routine—prayer journals, fasting, tithing, silent retreats, Bible study, accountability groups, healing prayer, constant direct contact with the poor, discussions of spiritual warfare, the presence or absence of God, genuine rage at God for those long stretches of absence."[36]

For me, it was the discussions of these regular practices that pulled me in closer to God. It filled a hunger I had for more, a deeper lifestyle of habits and patterns that scratched my itch, gave me a grip on following Jesus that I could keep. I never saw any of it as a path to earn God's acceptance, or atone for sin in my life, or become a member of the insider's club. I saw it as personal training to prepare myself, shape my life and future, create a new heart and soul, in the way an athlete shapes their life to meet the demands of the game.

♦ ♦ ♦ ♦ ♦

One Saturday morning, I enjoyed a bowl of nutty whole-grained cereal while solving the newspaper Sudoku puzzle and listening to an NPR Weekend Edition interview with musician, writer, and comic Stuart Davis. Davis mentioned during the interview that he has been a Buddhist practitioner for fifteen years. He said, "I have stayed with that path ever since then, and that is truly home."[37]

I wondered why we don't use language like that about following Jesus. Why don't I say, "I am a Christian practitioner—I have been following the path of Jesus for fifty-six years"? I'm comfortable to say I believe in Jesus; why is it uncomfortable to say I practice Christianity?

If I say I'm a practitioner, it implies a couple things: (1) my practices matter, and (2) I'm still learning. Saying I'm a practitioner puts the emphasis on what I do rather than what I say.

In a well-known Bible story, Jesus asked Peter, one of his closest friends and disciples, "Do you love me?" When Peter answered, "Yes," Jesus followed with the specific command, "Feed my sheep."[38]

In other words, don't just say you love me—do something about it. Don't just love, act. In other words, be a practitioner.

I live so much of my life inside my own head that it's easy for me to fall into the trap of believing that thinking about stuff has the same value as doing something. But the truth is, my practices matter.

If I say I love you but don't put you foremost in my life, I'm wrong—or lying. I cannot say I want to help you if all I do is talk, talk, talk. If my explanations smell more like excuses and justifications, then they smell, period. Jesus said, if you love me, take care of my people, love whom I love.

Being a practitioner of Christianity means I'm still learning. It means I don't yet know all the answers and I'm still searching for truth, still learning to walk like Jesus and, I hope, growing better and deeper every day.

One of my core beliefs is that we should grow closer to God every day. Another is that we should be lifelong students. Both of those beg for practice.

I read this (but unfortunately don't remember where): "The essence of Christianity is practicing the art of being His obedient children. A medical doctor, psychologist, teacher, professor, artist, and violinist are all considered practitioners of their occupation, vocation, and gift. Christ intends for us to be practitioners in action, service, and heart. The practice of the faith is truly from the heart and motivated by the love of Christ."

In Romans 12:1–2, Paul writes:

Take your everyday, ordinary life—your sleeping, eating, going-to-work, and walking-around life—and place it before God as an offering. Embracing what God does for you is the best thing you can do for him. Don't become so well-adjusted to your culture that you fit into it without even thinking. Instead, fix your attention on God. You'll be changed from the inside out. Readily recognize what he wants from you, and quickly respond to it. Unlike the culture around you, always dragging you down to its level of immaturity, God brings the best out of you, develops well-formed maturity in you." (MSG)

Those are good words. Living God's way takes a lot of practice.

Chapter 17

Still Learning New Tricks

My first time for this endoscopic adventure, they let me watch the procedure on a TV screen. It was fascinating to see inside my own insides, and I remember noticing how effectively I'd been cleansed. This time I stared at the screen waiting for the procedure to start, and then the nurse said I was finished, and it was time to wheel me out. I had slept through the whole thing.

It all started when we arrived at the Midland Memorial Hospital at 5:45 am and navigated labyrinthian hallways to the third-floor Endoscopy Department, named, apparently, because that is where they scope your end. We walked in the waiting room and were greeted by other people we knew, people too healthy to be in the hospital except for this particular age-triggered procedure. Smart humans get their first colonoscopy at age fifty, and then every ten years thereafter. Of course I stalled for two years and got mine at fifty-two, so here I was, ten years later at sixty-two, doing my family duty.

Young people who've never experienced a colonoscopy flinch when you tell them about it, but the procedure itself is painless and, other than going to the hospital at 6:00 a.m., trouble free. Experienced colonoscopites know the real discomfort is the foul potion they make you drink the day before, especially formulated by Professor Snape.

The evil brew comes in an almost empty gallon jug with about two inches of powder at the bottom, consisting of polyethylene glycol, sodium bicarbonate, sodium chlorate, and potassium chloride. You mix it with a gallon of water and then drink it one glass every ten minutes. They also include a small package of lemon flavoring, but its effect is marginal. I imagine the assembly line workers laughed as they attached the packets to the jugs.

I am usually skeptical of products advertised to cleanse organs. Maybe they work, but there isn't a sure way to know. That isn't the case with GaviLyte-N colonoscopy potion. It acts on the human body quickly, and its thoroughness is obvious.

When they first started the poking and sticking and measuring that goes with any hospital procedure, the nurse put a cuff on my arm, took my blood pressure, and wrote down the results. Since high blood pressure is one of my risk factors, I measure mine every morning, write it down, and of course enter it into Excel so I can plot a graph for my doctor. So this morning, naturally curious, I asked the nurse, "What did you get?"

"Oh, its normal."

That was a completely unsatisfactory answer. Even though he was kind and competent, I knew I could never be best friends with someone who wouldn't tell me the actual numbers when he had hard data in front of him.

But later, when they wheeled me into the endoscopy room and attached an EKG, I could see the digital readout. Nice touch, making the real time data visible. I was with my people.

My heartrate was lower than usual, 47 bpm, which told me the whole hospital experience hadn't made me nervous. That's good to know.

And then I had an idea, which brings me to the experiment Cyndi should have engaged with but didn't. Since I could see the digital heartrate readout, and since I was laying on the bed completely relaxed, and since I had nothing else to do until they rolled me over to get started, the game was on. How low could I push my heartrate?

In fact, I settled it down to 38 bpm, a personal record, before the alarm sounded and the nurses interfered with my game, or rather, experiment.

Later I tried to tell Cyndi how cool it was that I could change my body metrics by altering behavior, but she wasn't interested. It's a good thing she retired from teaching science so long ago or else I would worry about the quality of future leaders.

◆ ◆ ◆ ◆ ◆

Water was dripping from the ceiling in our guest bathroom. We knew it came from a leak in the roof. It only dripped during heavy rains, and we don't have any plumbing in the attic above this bathroom.

Fortunately for us, it seldom rains hard in West Texas, so the drip remained tiny and the damage to the sheetrock minimal. Unlike the time we returned to our mobile home from a two-week trip only to discover that an acoustic-type ceiling panel was sagging like a ready-to-burst-any-minute, upside-down balloon. This time the leak wasn't as potentially catastrophic.

After Cyndi pointed out the dripping ceiling, and then pointed it out again a week later, and once more the week after that (because sometimes I'm slow to engage in a project I don't like or didn't plan myself), I shifted into my home-handyman mode, which is to wait a bit longer still, allowing the problem ample time to repair itself. When that proved unsuccessful, I considered climbing up on the roof to identify any obvious damage, but I remembered the risk involved: Cyndi might find out.

When we first build this house and realized the roof would be too steep for someone like me to stand on, I suggested installing a giant eyebolt at the apex. "I could thread a rope through the bolt and belay myself when on the roof," I said. Cyndi quickly batted that plan away and said, in her sweetest voice, "I don't want you to ever go up on the roof. I need you to hang around a few more years."

I mostly obeyed until one December evening when I noticed a dozen Christmas lights along the eaves were burned out. They were scattered, meaning I'd have to move the ladder too many times to replace them, so I convinced myself climbing up on the roof was the smartest fix. However, as soon as I tried to stand on the slope I realized how much I'd underestimated (1) the height of our house, (2) the steepness of the roof, and (3) that Cyndi was probably right about staying off.

I laid down flat on the shingles, my head and arms toward the eaves, doing my best military belly crawl from bulb to bulb. When I dug into my pocket for the last bulb, I slid downward about two inches, enough to get my attention, enough that I could now peer over the edge. It occurred to me that if I kept sliding, the best outcome would be crashing headfirst into the thorny rose bushes, and the worst would be to bounce from the rose bushes onto the brick planter. I quickly replaced the bulb and climbed down and didn't mention the project to Cyndi, figuring she was smart enough to figure it out on her own.

About the leaking roof, I met the insurance appraiser, a fine young man, younger than either of my own children yet surely competent and experienced, who said the shingles all looked acceptable and the water was probably leaking through an aging and outdated bathroom vent. He composed a detailed, ten-page, itemized cost estimate that totaled to about 20 percent of our home insurance deductible.

I mentioned my project to the Iron Men on Thursday morning, along with a plan to climb up and pump a can of sealant into the leaks. I asked Cory, head physics teacher at Midland High School, to have his class calculate the coefficient of friction and recommend what I should wear while on the roof to minimize sliding risk. He said, knowing his class, they would recommend a Speedo.

Chad, owner of a commercial lumberyard who works with builders all day every day, asked if I planned to work up on the roof all by myself. He used that same incredulous expression I've seen at home, which communicated (1) he thought it was a bad idea, (2) I was a fool to consider it, and (3) he might've talked to Cyndi already.

Later that same day, Chad texted the personal phone number of the roofer who installed our roof ten years ago, along with this advice, "It's not expensive for his guys to fix a small vent." When I showed the text to Cyndi, she beamed with approval, confirming my suspicion of, if not conspiracy, certainly collusion with Chad.

Well, I met the roofer yesterday. He needed all of ten seconds to diagnose the problem and agree to repair it. He nodded his head in that experienced way, telling me I was smart to call him.

And so, what do I learn from all of this? Maybe that even after sixty years: (1) some decisions aren't easy, (2) it is hard to not assume I can do everything myself, even if I don't want to, and (3) being a responsible grown-up is a constant struggle.

Or, it could be the lesson I'm supposed to learn is that Cyndi is always right and I should do whatever she says. Whether that's true or not true, don't tell her I mentioned it. I'm counting on her not reading all the way to the end of this. She doesn't need to know everything.

♦ ♦ ♦ ♦ ♦

"I have been listening to the roots of my life," is what I said to Cyndi when I walked into our house. She smiled at me with that look she has whenever I say something like that. She's used to it.

"I've been driving around in my truck listening to some old lectures by Jim Rohn, and over and over I hear him say things that I first heard in 1983 that have imbedded into my life. Even as I listen, I am surprised. 'Oh, that's where I got that' I say to myself."

I recently bought a set of CDs by Rohn from 1981. I wanted those, rather than newer talks, so I could reconnect with the same words and language that first moved me to action.

Jim Rohn entered my life when I was at a crossroad. I was twenty-seven years old, married for four years, with a three-year-old son and newborn daughter. I was working as an engineer for a major company in a first-level manager position. I could have easily leaned back in satisfaction with the path I was on: slightly above-average work, slightly above-average schedule, slightly above-average TV every night, slightly above-average performance, providing slightly above-average parenting, and being a slightly above-average husband. I could have lived the next fifty years slightly above-average happy, ticking the right boxes, checking the right list, clicking off milestones, living a life of substance if not significance.

That isn't what happened. My friend Ricky loaned me a set of cassette tapes from a conference with Jim Rohn, and I listened and listened and listened. I took notes, and I took note.

In those days I heard a lot of motivational speakers, but none of them changed my life like Rohn. He was unusual in that he didn't talk much about dreaming or visualizing, or about "Whatever the mind of man can conceive, he can achieve," or about tapping the power within, or about overcoming fears by walking on hot coals. Rohn used to say, "You cannot grow strong on mental candy." His message was primarily about personal development and character. He showed me exactly what my slightly above-average self needed—the disciplines, practices, and habits that have stayed with me over thirty years.[39]

Sometime in the mid-1990s, my friend Bobby, who was instrumental in my twelve years in city government, told me, "You are not the same guy I first met ten years ago." He was right. I had Jim Rohn to thank for that.

Here are some things I learned in 1983 that still inform my life today:

Don't be a follower, be a student. When you hear a good idea, don't accept it at face value. Dive in and study it, learn it, make it your own. Don't be satisfied reading only one book on a topic, even if it's a best-seller. It might not be the right book.

Read two or three books to get a broader scope of the subject. Better yet, read four or five.

Set goals. Rohn said the greatest value in reaching goals is not the goal itself but who you become in order to attain it. I've set New Year's goals almost every year since then, and although I would guess my accomplishment rate is only about 30 percent, I'm a better man because of the efforts.

Casual living breeds casualties. I learned to be deliberate with my plans, intentional with my actions.

Capture wisdom. Write it down. We think we will remember the important stuff, but that is a lie. We won't remember anything we don't write down. I started my first journal in 1983, and my first entry was a poem by Shel Silverstein. The journal is full of lecture notes, song lyrics, Bible verses, and personal observations, and it was only the first of many. I never would have seen the wisdom as it passed by, much less captured it, if I hadn't learned the practice from Jim Rohn. He said, "You have to search for knowledge; rarely does a good idea interrupt you."

Keep a reading list. I've been a reader since I was very young, entering the library reading club every summer during my elementary school years. But Jim Rohn turned me into a systematic and aggressive reader. He said, "How sad if a man spends his book money on donuts. Ten years later he is overweight and behind in his life."

Rohn said the three treasures we should leave behind are photographs, a well-used library, and our personal journals. Since 1983, I have been working hard to accumulate all three.

♦ ♦ ♦ ♦ ♦

Wednesday morning, I dribbled my breakfast burrito down the front of my shirt. It was quite depressing. I've been feeding myself for a long time; a voice in my head tells me I should be past some of these problems.

As I drove away from the fine-dining establishment where I'd sat reading and writing and dribbling, I wondered whether I should go home first to change shirts. Had I still worked for the big corporation in an office filled with hopeful young adults, I would certainly have changed. I'd prefer not to be the old guy of the office, shuffling aimlessly among the cubicles in dirty clothes.

At a group at my church, I usually sit next to a man who is twenty years older than I am and wears predictable and persistent food stains on his black shirt. Sometimes the stains are new; sometimes the old ones disappear; but week after week, there are those stains. I don't want that to be people's memory of me. I don't want to be him.

But nowadays I work for a smaller, family-owned company, and just four of us are in the office on the busiest days. We are all in the same age group, meaning all of us have seen enough of life that we aren't easy to impress and we're hard to discourage. So I drove straight to the office without changing.

Besides, it wasn't a white shirt. It was dark blue, and since I sit behind a desk behind my computer screen all day, the salsa stain wouldn't be that obvious.

In my office building, I kept my portfolio across my chest while riding the elevator with well-dressed, stain-free, classy people. Once again, I didn't want to be that guy, even if I was that guy.

Later that day, during one of our frequent rambling office conversations, I learned that all three men working in the office had some sort of stain on their shirt, all from that morning. When I told my story and said I didn't worry about embarrassing my age group since everyone in the office was my age-group, my coworker Bob said, "And no one cares about your shirt. Isn't it great!"

Even the apostle Paul realized he wasn't yet who he hoped he'd be. He wrote in Romans 7, "I obviously need help! I realize that I don't have what it takes [to do good]. I can will it, but I can't do it. I decide to do good, but I don't really do it; I decide not to do bad, but then I do it anyway. My decisions, such as they are, don't result in actions. Something has gone wrong deep within me and gets the better of me every time" (vv. 17–20 MSG).

Here's the thing about this story. Maybe what we offer the world isn't a perfect life, a pristine story, or even a clean shirt. Perfect people have little effect on the world, and few people listen to their advice. Their story is too unbelievable and their advice unfollowable, if not completely irrelevant.

When we read the Bible, we see that time after time God chose to work with those who limped through life wearing stained clothes. We are in good company.

Fortunately, I don't dribble food on my clothes every day. I hope I have a stain-free shirt when you and I meet. But if I'm holding my portfolio across my chest, just don't ask. Let me shuffle on my way to the old guy's section.

♦ ♦ ♦ ♦ ♦

As I write this, I'm 21,901 days old. The reason I know this is, I followed Psalm 90:12, which tells us to "number our days, that we may gain a heart of wisdom." I used Excel to count the days since I didn't have time to count the pages on a calendar.

What does 21,901 days mean? It means I'm 59.96 years old, firmly perched on the line of my sixtieth year. Being true to my analytical self, I've been trying to understand the significance of this.

When I turned fifty, people asked if it bothered me. In fact, it made me happy. It was a relief to no longer feel the pressure to be cool or stylish or hip. I went straight for eccentric, which is much more fun.

But that was 9.96 years ago; what about now? What do I expect when I turn sixty? Who will I become?

Naturally, I did a Google search on the number sixty to see what showed up. I learned there are four Archimedean solids with sixty vertices. The most interesting one, in my opinion, is the truncated icosahedron (think of a soccer ball, with thirty-two faces, ninety edges, and sixty vertices). It has the best potential for a birthday cake, or it would if I was a cake guy. I would rather have Cyndi's homemade apple pie than a birthday cake, no matter what the shape.

I learned that the Latin term sexagena refers to five dozen, or sixty, and was the typical ransom for a captured Teutonic knight.

I read about the Babylonians, who used a base-sixty numbering system. Since I usually confuse myself when calculating non-base-ten numbers, I asked my go-to expert in all things, Daryl Jensen, whether my Babylonian age would be one or ten. He wrote back, "If you were to translate Babylonian symbols to Arabic numerals, you would actually be 10. However, even that is problematic since the Babylonians had no symbol for 0. My understanding is that the difference between 1 and 60 (which would look identical using Babylonian symbols) had to be inferred from context."

I'm sure if you hang out with me, you'll get the context.

The Bible says in Genesis 25:26 that Isaac was sixty years old when his twin sons, Jacob and Esau, were born. Fortunately, Cyndi and I have put the birthing of babies behind us.

Sports cars are rated by how long it takes them to go from zero to sixty miles an hour. I don't know what to do with this info, though, since I've never been an accelerator but a steady stater.

I read too many magazine articles about how sixty is the new forty (or even the new thirty), but I've never heard any thirty- or forty-year-olds say this. In fact, I don't want to be forty again. I am much more comfortable with my place in life, more comfortable in my own skin now than twenty years ago. When I turned forty, life was too scary and uncertain.

The same magazine articles like to point out that seventy has replaced sixty as the normal retirement age. Maybe so. I'm afraid I would be bored if I completely retired from working—probably hole up in my cave and never come out. Cyndi once told me my writing gets narrow and shallow when I'm not around people, working. If she's correct, and she usually is, I should keep working as long as I plan to keep writing. That's a long time.

I learned the number sixty represents the global Karma of the Universe, but I have no idea what that means, and I don't plan to study it any further.

Bible Gateway reminded me that the gold statue king Nebuchadnezzar commissioned, the same one that got Daniel in trouble, was sixty cubits high. I won't be building a sixty-cubit statue of myself. That's too creepy. And besides, Nebuchadnezzar is a particularly lousy role model to follow.

♦ ♦ ♦ ♦ ♦

Early one Friday morning, Cyndi and I noticed one of our two pistache trees leaning against our house. I was driving home from early morning weight-lifting class at the gym and caught the nonvertical anomaly in my peripheral vision.

It had apparently rotted from the roots just below ground level. The trunk was not broken but leaning at the surface, and there was no disturbance of the ground around it. It was still attached to its own root system on one side. Since the tree seemed somewhat stable in its lean and wasn't hurting the house, we left it alone for the time being since we had to drive to Cloudcroft, New Mexico, for a family wedding.

That Sunday afternoon, once we were back at home, our friend and tree-whisperer, Miles, came over to look at the tree and give advice. He confirmed our fears. The tree was a goner. Even though the leaves were still green, its days were limited. He said we could straighten it up and stake it vertical, but it would fall again someday, and it might be bigger, and it might land on something or someone we care about.

Since we were several months away from planting season, we decided to leave our leaning tree the way it was for a while. At least it was throwing off shade.

And then the next Wednesday night, a fierce storm blew through the neighborhood. Thursday morning we noticed the tree was still standing, but it was now leaning a different direction, against the porch. It seemed more unstable than before. It was time to take it down.

Remarkably, with no regard to my personal history, in full optimism I borrowed a chainsaw from Clark. I say all that because my experience with chainsaws is that they don't run when I'm holding them. Maybe they work all day for you but not for me. It is a glaring hole in my man card.

I tried to cut down the tree that Friday afternoon, but even though Clark's chainsaw was almost new, used only once, I couldn't get it started. I even put in a new spark plug, drained the fuel and replaced it, read the manual and followed all the steps. No joy.

My across-the-alley neighbor, Randy, saw my dilemma and loaned his electric chainsaw. I was able to start it, but smoke poured out of the motor, so I returned it before I destroyed it.

We borrowed another electric chainsaw from Cyndi's sister, Tonya, but by then it was too dark to do anything safely, so I decided to attack the tree the next day after my bike ride.

Saturday morning I rode fifty miles, arriving back home about noon completely full of myself as a cyclist and as a manly man, only to discover my tree had been cut down and the branches piled on the sidewalk near the street. Some lumberjack elves (I was going to say wood elves, but no one likes wood elves) did the job for me.

I went to eat lunch and recover from my ride; I wanted to do some writing before hauling away the tree branches. But afterward, when I drove up to my house, there was Randy and his son pulling away. They had put all the branches in Randy's pickup and were about to haul them off. I barely arrived in time to catch them. Randy jumped out of his truck, shook my hand, I told him thanks, and he took off to finish his good deed.

Besides being a good guy, a great neighbor, and the friend we all hope to have, I think Randy fixed my problem partly because he felt sorry for me. Cyndi told him I was a chainsaw loser, so he took care of me.

Letting other people help you is often the hardest thing in the world. Being reminded of your limitations is not pleasant. It's hard being the one who needs help. It doesn't seem very leaderly. We are more comfortable giving than receiving. It is hard to accept help, even harder than admitting chainsaw incompetence.

One of the things I've learned these past few years is how I overrated self-sufficiency in my younger years. I considered it one of my best features, proud that I could sneak through life without asking or needing much from anyone else.

It was a mistake to think that way. We must be willing to receive if we expect to know the grace of God. Only empty-handed people can understand grace.

♦ ♦ ♦ ♦ ♦

I've spent most of my life being afraid of messing up, making the big mistake, falling on my face, looking foolish, like an amateur, silly and insignificant. I didn't want to regret my actions.

Now in my midsixties, I'm much more afraid of the regrets of inaction. I'm becoming less afraid of messing up and more afraid of missing out. I don't want to end up old and dried up, wishing I had been brave enough to try stuff but didn't because I was afraid of failing.

I like what the apostle Paul wrote in 2 Corinthians 6:1: "Please don't squander one bit of this marvelous life God has given us" (MSG). I don't want to squander.

I've wondered if my change of attitude is some sort of midlife crisis, where I worry about unaccomplished goals more than I worry about public failure. Or maybe it's because the longer I live, the lengthier is my list of mistakes survived, and the greater my confidence for future recovery and survival. Or because I see the window of opportunity slowly closing, and I know I have to make my move now in order to have time to get it done.

I think the biggest lesson I've learned is the futility of waiting until I am prepared and ready before moving forward. I now know that I'll never be prepared enough, or ready enough, for anything.

So my new plan is to sign up for the race sooner; commit to the adventure right away; agree to help Cyndi now, not later; and stop wasting so much time worrying about my preparations. Too often I've used my need for preparation as an excuse to never get started.

Don't get me wrong. I'm not becoming the sort of guy who dives into things without planning ahead. I doubt I'll become more spontaneous as I get older—I'll still live by checklists and spreadsheets, and I'll still research my options before undertaking a new adventure. I'll still put a lot of energy into preparation. But I won't let the blank spots immobilize me. I've been preparing sixty years to be prepared enough to move forward without 100 percent preparation.

Chapter 18

What We Learned from a Good Dog

In Lady the Running Labrador, Cyndi and I got exactly the dog we needed. She lived with us twelve and a half years, ran thousands of miles with us, and in her own fashion, wriggled her way into the hearts of two non-dog-people in the most subtle ways. She taught us how to live with love and grace during her final years and how to grow old with dignity and value.

Lady is gone now. She died Saturday afternoon, August 28, 2010, on the table at the vet's office. But her influence on Cyndi and me still lingers ten years later. I expect it will last the rest of our lives.

When Lady joined our family in 1998, she immediately fit in, partly because she was so undemanding. She lived lightly among us. She entertained herself and didn't want much attention.

That was perfect since we have never been overly accommodating people. We expect everyone in the house to make their own way, pick up their own stuff, take care of their own clothes, eat what everyone else eats, carry their own stuff in from the car, and heal themselves when sick. We have been accused of being the no-mercy family, and it is true that when Cyndi and I have taken those spiritual gifts surveys, mercy ends up at the bottom of both our lists, but we try not to be mean or judgmental. We just expect each person to pull up their pants and take care of their own stuff. Lady fit right in with us.

When we got her, I was looking for a dog to run with Cyndi and Katie to keep them safe. I was looking for a black Lab because they appear mean, even when they aren't. A running dog doesn't have to be attack-trained to protect a runner—any dog will keep almost all attackers away.

I spent time on the internet searching for the best breed for running, finally settling on either a greyhound or a Labrador retriever. They both seemed to be good with people. I preferred a greyhound because I thought the idea of rescuing a racing dog was a cool idea and because all greyhounds love to run. From what I read, Labradors were iffier. Some loved to run, some didn't, and you couldn't tell by looking at them. And some Labs suffered from hip dysplasia that made running impossible.

I found someone south of town who owned greyhounds, and I drove Katie down to see them. She was a bit shocked to see these two dogs who were as tall as she was (Katie was a freshman in high school at the time). She thought they were funny looking, long and lean and skinny and strong. I thought that was a good description of Katie as well.

Since the greyhound idea went nowhere, I called the city animal control office and told the director I was looking for a gentle black Lab who could run with us. The man called back a few days later and said he had a black Lab for us to look at, but he also knew of a yellow Lab (mix) that was being kept temporarily by a friend. The dog had been lost or abandoned, no collar or tags, and the woman didn't want to send the dog to animal control, knowing its fate if no one adopted her.

Cyndi and Katie and I drove over to the house and went into the backyard to play with the big yellow Lab. She wasn't pure Lab, had some other breeds mixed in her bloodlines. At one point I asked the home owner if she thought this dog would adopt to a new family, and the woman pointed across the porch to where Cyndi and Katie were sitting on the concrete and the Lab was lying across their laps. I knew we were taking this dog home that day.

I thought we should call our big, beautiful new dog Goldie since it described her so well. Cyndi said, "Katie and I want to call her Lady." I said this dog would be a great outside dog and Cyndi said, "Except for nighttime. She should spend nights inside with us." I realized that even though this project to find a running dog was my idea and my initiative and all my work, I had been cleanly excised from the process and from now on I would be a bystander.

We learned some things about Lady right away. She didn't like being in water deeper than her belly, and she showed no interest in fetching anything (most Labrador retrievers love these things). She didn't seem to care much about playing or wrestling. She seldom barked, and she never barked inside the house. She never made a mess in the house. She only dug in the backyard to find a cool place to lie down, and even then she was discrete about her digging locations. She never chewed anything she wasn't supposed to chew. She mostly laid around on the floor and licked the carpet.

And she loved to run.

I realize that all dogs like to run around the backyard, but that isn't what I mean. Lady loved to go for two miles, or five miles, or sometimes ten or twelve miles. She simply loved it. She could tell when anyone in the house was getting dressed to go running, and she would dance in the hallway.

Lady knew the difference between our getting ready to run versus getting ready to work in the yard—either of which involved wearing shorts and T-shirts. Cyndi thought Lady was keying off our shoes. I wasn't so sure since. I had a closet full of old running shoes retired from the road but active in the garage and yard. How could she tell dirty running shoes from dirty yard shoes when they were both the same model of New Balances? I don't know. But she knew. And when she detected a run coming up, she'd start jumping and hopping, and she'd stay very close so she wouldn't be left behind. If the bedroom door was closed and she was in the hallway and knew one of us was getting ready to run, she would bump her head into the door over and over to make sure we knew she wanted to go.

It was the only time in her life that she showed excitement, and she was completely over-the-top. Lacing up our running shoes often was hard with Lady right in our faces, jumping and smiling and . . . well, being overjoyed.

Lady ran daily with one or more members of our family for ten years—literally thousands of miles. She never complained if we asked her to run twice in a day, or if it was raining, or cold, or if the spring wind was howling. She was always ready to go.

Our regular five-mile route took us around the pathways of C. J. Kelly Park. Cyndi and her friend Meta ran with Lady very early in the morning before the sun came up, usually off-leash since no one else was out.

I ran with her between 5:30 and 6:00 p.m., always on the leash since the park was filled with kids practicing sports. Lady didn't care about kids in the park or balls bouncing by or rolling past. She was in her own running world, and all distractions were nonexistent to her. If she was off-leash, she would run huge arcs, paying attention to everything; but when running on the leash, she was focused and tunnel visioned. I don't know how many times a soccer ball or baseball would come rolling across in front of us, sometimes right into our path. Lady didn't care and didn't respond except to quickly hop over the rolling ball. She never even turned her head.

She was the same with other dogs in the park. They could run around, or bark, or growl—Lady never gave them the courtesy of acknowledgment. She was on her mission. She had five miles to run. She was a dog at work and would not be distracted or delayed.

My earliest documented run with her was a five-miler through Grasslands on May 13, 1998. I don't know if Cyndi or Katie ran with her before I did (they didn't keep detailed running logs of their own). For years I ran with her two or three times a week during the evenings. For even more years and more miles, Cyndi ran with Lady in the early mornings and on long runs on the weekends. In her prime, it was nothing for Lady to go ten or twelve miles with Cyndi every Saturday morning.

Eventually Lady got too old to run more than a few blocks. However, she still wanted to go, and she would get so excited when she knew either of us was getting dressed to run. We felt guilty leaving her behind because she wanted to go so badly. But she was no longer capable. There were times when we carried our running gear out into the garage to change where she couldn't see us, then sneaked out the garage door to go run without her.

As Lady got older, losing much of her vision and hearing, she also got more and more "in the way." She laid on the floor at our feet all the time. She slept on the floor of our bedroom right next to one of us, right where we put our feet if we got up at night, making a big target for tripping in the middle of the night. We adjusted to her being underfoot, and in fact, we liked it. She still didn't care much to be petted or rubbed, but she wanted to be close to us. It was sweet and tender to watch her follow us around the house.

She was always independent, self-contained, and content with minimal attention from us. To pet her, you had to be the one to cross the room, and you had to get your rubbing in before she got tired of the whole thing and wandered off to be by herself. On many occasions when she saw me drop my hands in an invitation for her to come get her ears rubbed, I could tell she was weighing in her mind whether it was worth the walk across the room. She'd decide it wasn't and lie down on the floor looking off in the other direction. My brother, Carroll, once described her during a late-night telephone conversation about our dogs: "Lady is a working dog, not a lap dog."

She wouldn't push herself on anyone. She wouldn't beg for attention (although she might beg for an occasional pizza crust), or jump in your lap, or expect you to play with her. Sometimes I wished she were more aggressive in seeking my affection, so I wouldn't feel guilty about ignoring her or taking her for granted.

She wanted to be in the same room, but she typically laid down facing away. Her eyes might be open, but she showed no interest in watching the people in the room. One day I said to

Cyndi, "It's as if she wants to be with us but she's too cool to act like she needs us. So she lies down close and then stares the other direction. It's like having a teenager in the house again."

Cyndi disagreed. "No, she's being part of our family without placing demands on us. She's doing what she's always done."

And then Cyndi said, "But she's taught us to be more accommodating and gentler around her."

Cyndi was correct. We were more careful when we opened doors, or scooted back in our chairs, or lowered the footrest to the recliner. Instead of getting mad that she was always in the way, we were happy for her gentleness and happy to step around her.

I can't count how many times she laid down against the back legs of my chair so I couldn't scoot back to go refill my drink but had to crawl out of the chair sideways, or against the shower door so Cyndi couldn't open it to get her towel, or against the door to the garage so we bumped into her when we got home and came inside. She would lie down under the library table so there was not enough room for our feet. Maybe this was her way of interacting with us. She wouldn't play, so she got in the way.

Lady used to lie down directly under the elevated footrest when I was sitting in my recliner, so close that I couldn't lower the chair without mashing her. I would have to crawl over the arms of the chair to keep from disturbing her. To be honest, I was surprised at my own tolerance of Lady. I guess I loved the whole package of her, good and bad, easy or inconvenient. In fact, not only did I tolerate her under my chair but I missed her if she was in the other room.

I remember one night when I woke up about 1:30 a.m. and couldn't go back to sleep, so I grabbed my book and glasses and moved to the living room couch. Lady came along with me (she had been sleeping at the foot of our bed). She curled up on the floor beside the couch near my head and went back to sleep. About every twenty minutes, she sat up and laid her chin on the couch and on my book to see what was going on. Maybe she was getting a closer look at me, or maybe she was checking in, or maybe she knew I had been restless and couldn't sleep, and she was offering the best comfort she had without intruding.

By the time we moved to our current house in Woodland Park, Lady had lived and run with us for ten years. She was too frail to run at all, and she knew it. She didn't press to go along. But she loved her twice-daily walks through the park. Toward the end, her back legs were so weak and frail she would hobble along, often sitting to rest a couple times before finishing the walk.

I once spent a weekend at home by myself, placing books on the shelves, carrying boxes from the garage, and putting stuff in my closet. Every time I changed rooms, Lady followed me and curled up on the floor. But I was moving from room to room a lot, and she had to get up to follow and then curl up again, and then get up to follow again, over and over. None of it looked comfortable. I started feeling guilty that she was moving so often, and I tried to bunch my trips more. I even tried to sneak out of the room one time. I realized what a strange situation it was, that I was worried about inconveniencing her and all she wanted to do was hang out with me.

There has been some dispute regarding Lady's actual age. She was a full-sized dog when we first got her in the spring of 1998. At her first visit, the vet guessed her birthday to be 1993 based on her teeth; however, that means she was seventeen years old when she died, or 50 percent older than her expected life span. A month before her death, we were at our annual vet visit, and Dr. Sheele said she was the oldest dog in his practice. He also said she had great heart and lungs.

The last time I took her on a walk was Friday morning the day before she died, and she was barely mobile. She looked like a loose bag of bones. I sat on one of the park benches and stared into her eyes; she seemed to be telling me she was tired and ready to be done. Enough was enough.

Through the years, my relationship with Lady often reminded me of my relationship with God. Like God, Lady wasn't pushy and wasn't aggressive, even when I wanted her to be. She waited for me to make the first move, but even then, she was always nearby. All she wanted to do was hang out with us and love on us in her fashion. And the longer our time together, the more I valued our walks outside. I guess I just wanted to take care of her in my own fashion, as she had taken care of me all these years.

Cyndi and I have never been true dog lovers, but Lady ran her way into our lives. It is impossible to imagine those twelve years without her and impossible to share so many miles with anyone—dog or person—without growing affection. In her final years, she taught us about grace and how important it was to make room in our hearts for each other. The inconveniences weren't meant to be inconvenient; they were questions: Do you still have room for me?

Lady was on my mind one morning when I read from my Daily Bible. Psalm 27:4 says,

> *One thing I ask of the Lord,*
> *this only do I seek:*

> *that I may dwell in the house of the Lord*
> *all the days of my life,*
> *to gaze on the beauty of the Lord*
> *and to seek him in his temple.*

The Message says, "I'll study at his feet." Isn't that sweet?

What did we learn from a good dog? We learned how to grow old in grace, love, and affection. How to find new ways of engaging with those we love even as our physical abilities deteriorate. We learned the value of simply being close to someone. I want to live with God that same way. I want to live my life all the way to the end, just like Lady.

Epilogue

Leaning Forward

When is it OK to settle in life, and when should we press on? Settling doesn't always mean giving up. It's often a sign of contentment, the balance between effort and results. Settling also opens space in life for new things. We can't press hard on everything; we settle in some areas to clear room for others.

And yet, the older I am, the less I desire to settle. Maybe it's more accurate to say I'm afraid to settle.

I've adopted a line from Robert Frost as my Six-Word Memoir: Miles to go before I sleep. It's from a poem about a man who enjoys the beauty of snow falling in the woods but must travel on. No matter how nice the feeling, there were promises to keep, people to help, obligations to fulfill, and dreams to be dreamed.

Therein is my dilemma. Do I slow down and enjoy the peace and beauty of a gentle life, or do I press on because . . . I have miles to go before I sleep.

♦ ♦ ♦ ♦ ♦

This is how I want to live . . .

Widened circles
Greater differentiation
Larger viewpoints
Greater inclusivity
Deeper understanding
More honest
Bigger God
Bigger places
Freedom to change my mind
Leaning forward

And yet, as I hope to continue expanding and filling all the rest of my days, I also want to narrow my focus and my message, pare down the things I do, so that they all point toward, contribute to, this: guiding people to a deeper life with God; telling stories that put truth within reach.

Simultaneous expansion and contraction.

That's what I want.

♦ ♦ ♦ ♦ ♦

When I say I am a lifelong pilgrim in search of God, I wonder, am I initiating this or am I following? Am I pulling on a chain, or am I hanging on to a chain that's pulling me?

The older I get, the more I feel it pulling me. So many things that are deep spiritual experiences for me now weren't even part of my life ten to twenty years ago. Not only were they not a part, but I avoided them.

♦ ♦ ♦ ♦ ♦

Here's the point: I don't want settling to be my default pattern. I don't want to end up one of those old men yearning for the past. I am tired of stories about the good old days. I want to lean forward into the future. I have promises to keep.

♦ ♦ ♦ ♦ ♦

I read a book by Eugene Peterson titled *A Long Obedience in the Same Direction*. That describes how I want to live and who I want to be.

By temperament and personality, I'm a man of stability and momentum. I don't get tired of doing the same things the same way for a long time. I don't fear or resist change, but I see little need for change simply for the sake of changing. I need a reason.

I was a long-distance runner, never a sprinter. I am a long-distance cyclist, not a sprinter. I think about life like a marathoner, holding a sustainable pace and covering long distance. I grow suspicious of quick answers or immediate solutions.

I believe daily practices, even seemingly mundane ones like walking a mile around the pond every day, change your life. They rewire our brains, help us solve problems, and open our perception of the world. The simple repetition molds us. It often puts our brains on autopilot, which opens us up for creativity and imagination.

♦ ♦ ♦ ♦ ♦

One of my favorite quotes came from a friend of songwriter Rich Mullins: "What window was he looking out of?" He said that because Rich saw God in places no one else noticed.

I like the image of pulling back the curtain to a big picture window to show how much more there is. The view always gets bigger. There is always more.

As I get older, I quickly lose interest in things that don't get bigger the longer I look. I want to be involved in deeper, bigger things, ideas, movements. I don't want to waste the time I have left quibbling over small ideas.

♦ ♦ ♦ ♦ ♦

Listening to an audio book titled *The Last Battle*, by C. S. Lewis, I heard this conversation:

"I see," she said at last, thoughtfully. "I see now. This garden is like the Stable. It is far bigger inside than it was outside."

"Of course, Daughter of Eve," said the faun. "The further in you go, the bigger everything gets. The inside is larger than the outside."[40]

I was so moved by this exchange that I pulled my analog version of the book off my shelf so I could copy this passage accurately.

The notion that things can be bigger on the inside than on the outside is why I keep diving into music, why I love cycling and running and thru-hiking, why I like epic adventures. I want to go further into the things I enjoy, knowing that the further in I go, the bigger they will be.

I want to invest my years on topics that are bigger on the inside than on the outside. I don't have much interest in studying concepts that can be learned quickly or mastered overnight.

I want to know that the more I learn, the more there is, and that the more I know, the less I know.

I want to immerse my life in things that get bigger the further in I go.

I long for the inside (of me) to be larger than the outside.

About the Author

Berry Simpson has published four books: Running With God, Retreating With God, Remodeled, and Trail Markers. In addition, he's written a weekly blog since 1998, as well as numerous magazine articles.

When he isn't writing in the corner booth of his favorite fast-food restaurant, Whataburger (a Texas icon), he spends his time reading, running, cycling, backpacking, teaching, playing trombone, and loving his wife Cyndi. They've been married since July 1979, have two adult children, Byron and Katherine, and two granddaughters, Madden and Landry.

Berry has taught adult Bible classes at his church for the past thirty years and leads an early morning men's book study class - Iron Men.

He received a Bachelor of Science degree in Petroleum Engineering from the University of Oklahoma and has solved problems for a variety of energy companies for over forty years.

Keep in touch with Berry and find more of his writing at his website: www.berrysimpson.com, or on Facebook: www.facebook.com/BerrySimpsonAuthor

Notes

[1] David Brooks, *The Second Mountain: A Quest for a Moral Life* (New York: Random House, 2019), xii.

[2] See Paisano Baptist Encampment website, http://www.paisanoencampment.org/.

[3] See Glorieta Adventure Camps website, https://glorieta.org/.

[4] See the OUBCM website, http://www.oubcm.com/.

[5] The Message (MSG).

[6] Leo Cooney in Sherwin B. Nuland, *The Art of Aging: A Doctor's Prescription for Well-Being* (New York: Random House, 2007), 144.

[7] Leonard Sweet, *Soul Salsa: Seventeen Surprising Steps For Godly Living in the Twenty-First Century* (Grand Rapids: Zondervan, 2000), 17.

[8] Sweet, *Soul Salsa*, 18.

[9] William Broyles Jr. and Al Reinert, *Apollo 13,* Universal Pictures, 1995.

[10] Dean Karnazes, *Ultra Marathon Man: Confessions of an All-Night Runner* (New York: Penguin, 2006), 107.

[11] Seth Godin, *Poke the Box: When Was the Last Time You Did Something for the First Time?* (New York: Portfolio/Penguine, 2015), 64.

[12] Sloane Crosley, *I Was Told There'd Be Cake: Essays* (New York: Riverhead, 2008), 225–28.

[13] Mark Rowlands, *Running with the Pack: Thoughts from the Road on Meaning and Mortality* (New York: Pegasus, 2014), 19.

[14] Rowlands, *Running with the Pack*, 20.

15. Kathleen Norris, *Dakota: A Spiritual Geography* (New York: Houghton Mifflin, 1993), 130.

16. Barbara Kingsolver, *Small Wonder: Essays* (New York: Harper Perennial, 2003), 40.

17. Scott Jurek, *North: Finding My Way While Running the Appalachian Trail* (New York: Little Brown and Co., 2018), 277.

18. *A Walk in the Woods*, Route One Films, 2015.

19. Louis L'Amour, *Education of a Wandering Man: A Memoir* (New York: Bantam, 1989), 48.

20. John Claypool, *Tracks of a Fellow Struggler: Living and Growing through Grief* (Harrisburg, NY: Morehouse, 1974), 8.

21. Check it out! *BDS Cartoon Collection*, https://www.facebook.com/BDS-Cartoon-Collection-407905952963194.

22. *August Rush*, Southpaw Entertainment, 2007.

23. Madeline Burser, *The Art of Practicing: A Guide to Making Music from the Heart* (New York: Three Rivers Press, 1997), 228.

24. Twyla Tharp, *Keep It Moving: Lessons for the Rest of Your Life* (New York: Simon & Schuster, 2019), 123.

25. John Ortberg, *Soul Keeping: Caring for the Most Important Part of You* (Grand Rapids: Zondervan, 2014), 73.

26. Paul Miller, *A Praying Life: Connecting With God in a Distracting World* (Colorado Springs: NavPress, 2009), 11.

27. C. S. Lewis, *The Lion, the Witch, and the Wardrobe* (New York: Collier Books, 1950), 159.

28. Henri Nouwen, *With Open Hands*, 2nd. ed. (Notre Dame, IN: Ave Maria Press, 2006).

29. Alex Sparks, "The Origin Story," blog for Keep Exploring website, April 22, 2019, https://www.wekeepexploring.com/blogs/the-origin-story/the-origin-story.

30. Sarah Gordon, "'World's oldest backpacker' plans two-month trip to Europe at 95 years old," *Daily Mail*, May 11, 2012, https://www.dailymail.co.uk/travel/article-2142863/Worlds-oldest-backpacker-set-month-trip-Europe-95-years-

old.html#:~:text=Australian%20backer%20Keith%20Wright%20loves,globetrotter%20is%2095%20years%20old.

[31] Oliver Sacks, *Gratitude* (New York: Knopf, 2016) 9.

[32] Sacks, *Gratitude*, 10.

[33] 1 Corinthians 9:27 NASB.

[34] Philip Yancey, *Reaching for the Invisible God: What Can We Expect to Find?* (Grand Rapids: Zondervan, 2000),169.

[35] Mark Batterson, *If: Trading Your* If Only *Regrets for God's* What If *Possibilities* (Grand Rapids: Baker, 2015), 53.

[36] David Brooks, *The Second Mountain: The Quest for a Moral Life* (New York: Random House, 2019), 241.

[37] Stuart Davis, "Stuart Davis on 'Sex, God, Rock 'n Roll,'" *NPR Weekend Edition*, interview by Scott Simon, May 16, 2009, https://www.npr.org/templates/story/story.php?storyId=104211900.

[38] See John 21:15–17.

[39] The tapes by Jim Rohn were from a business convention whose date and location have disappeared into the ages past. I had copies of copies which, regretfully, I wore out long ago.

[40] C. S. Lewis, *The Last Battle* (New York: Collier Books, 1956), 180.

www.ingramcontent.com/pod-product-compliance
Lightning Source LLC
Chambersburg PA
CBHW051943290426
44110CB00015B/2084